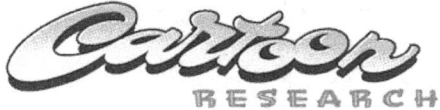
Presents

Winsor McCay's
THE SINKING
OF
THE ALPENA

Written and Compiled
By
Kevin Scott Collier

Winsor McCay's
THE SINKING OF THE ALPENA

By Kevin Scott Collier

All entries attributed to John Canemaker © 2005 John Canemaker

Presented by

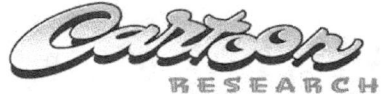

827 North Hollywood Way #100

Burbank, California 91505

Visit us online:

www.cartoonresearch.com

Founder: Jerry Beck

Email: jerrybeck18@gmail.com

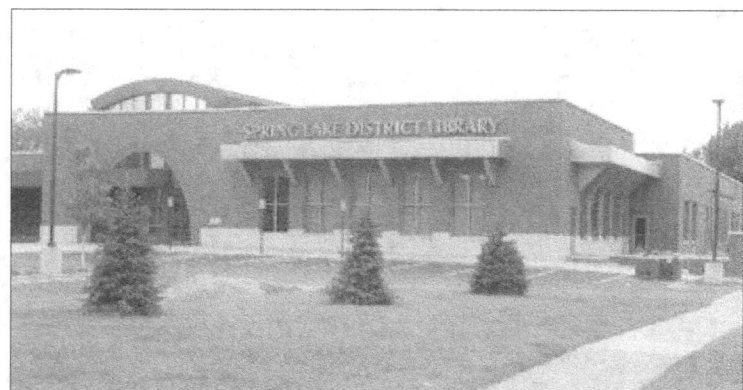

Special thanks to the Spring Lake District Library, Michigan.

Winsor McCay's The Sinking of The Alpena, written by Kevin Scott Collier. Copyright Kevin Scott Collier. Presented and available through Cartoon Research. Special thanks to The Tri-Cities Historical Museum. Sources: Ottawa County records. Spring Lake District Library. Issues of Spring Lake's *The Republican* newspaper 1879-80. Tri-Cities Historical Museum. Spring Lake historical books and documents. Spring Lake District Library. Historical papers from of Spring Lake individuals. The Library of Congress newspaper collection. Special thanks to John Canemaker.

FOREWORD
By Kevin Scott Collier

Three miles from my residence is the location of Winsor McCay's boyhood home and school he attended. Both structures are long since gone, but the parcel of land where Union School once stood is designated as Winsor McCay Park. On it is a historical marker designating Spring Lake as the childhood home of pioneering animator and cartoonist Winsor McCay.

While born in Canada on September 26, 1867, his home for the first 18 years of his life, 1867-1885, was Spring Lake.

The McCay Park lot has an interesting feature buried in the grass. Portions of the cement foundation of Union School, which burned down after the McCays departed Spring Lake, is visible. If you stand in the center, you are inside the virtual school. And, you are standing on the location where Winsor McCay, at the age of 13, drew his very first "commercial" illustration, *The Sinking of The Alpena*.

Yes, before there was McCay's *Sinking of The Lusitania*, there was a steamer that went down in Lake Michigan. It was the subject of a chalkboard illustration McCay created on his classroom blackboard.

A photographer took a photo of it and prints were sold, a cut going to young McCay. The image has been stored away by the Ottawa County, Michigan historical resources for over a century. In fact, they didn't even know what they had. To them it was a chalkboard drawing of a ship that sank in 1880 that had "local" significance, not national.

There are many great books written on the career of comic strip artist and pioneering animator Winsor McCay. The Spring Lake District Library, next to Winsor McCay Park, has assembled virtually all of them for the public to enjoy. On the 150th anniversary of his birthday, September 26, 2017, the library will put on display a large, framed print of McCay's *The Sinking of The Alpena*.

Folks in Spring Lake know McCay grew up here. I've personally lectured on McCay in Spring Lake, and in the neighboring Ottawa county, for 35 years.

I approached this book no differently from the many local history books I have written. I have combed the archives of our county for decades, and for many years wrote a local history column weekly for the newspaper. I probably have run across the history, census entries, and birth or death certificates

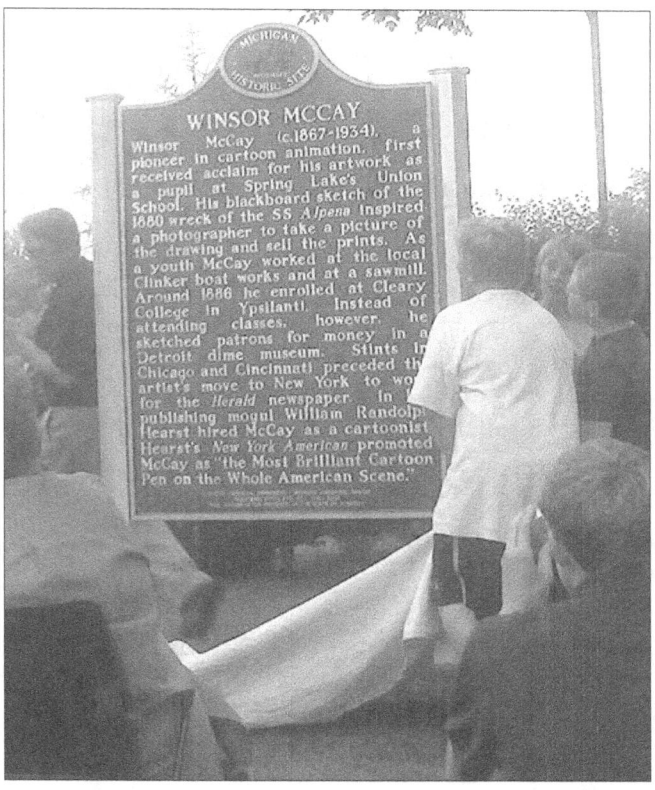

The Winsor McCay historical marker, unveiled in 2008, at the Winsor McCay Park, Spring Lake, Michigan.

of most everyone who ever lived in our area.

Obviously McCay is a world-wide phenomenon, but when it's local in origination, you know where to look. And if you don't, you know someone who does.

Spring Lake's Winsor McCay Committee meets regularly, usually once a month. We work on ideas for the development of the park, and also plan the annual McCay Day event held every June at the Spring Lake District Library. I even teach a cartooning class at the event. Spring Lake artist Aaron Zenz shows up, too, and creates McCay related stuff with the kids.

It's time to dust off the old photo taken of young Winsor McCay's *The Sinking of The Alpena* drawing, and present it for his fans to enjoy for the first time in its' full size glory.

This book also explains McCay's birth year and presents the possibility that a local childhood event had a part in the creation of the Little Nemo character. Also included are never before published photos of McCay's school and a glimpse of his boyhood home. Enjoy the journey!

WINSOR McCAY'S BIRTH YEAR
How A Spring Lake Census Taker Tripped Up Historians

Winsor Zenas McCay's birth year has been a subject of dispute ever since he died on July 26, 1934, because no birth records or certificates exist.

Compounding the mystery was McCay himself, whom, after departing his parent's home as a young adult, began to manipulate his birth year, bumping it to 1869, and later to 1871.

"He probably fiddled with the year out of vanity, or to reduce the age difference between himself and his much younger wife," author John Canemaker explained for the purpose of this book.

It appears that was indeed the case.

Winsor McCay met Maude Leonore Dufour in 1891, when he was working in Cincinnati, Ohio. After a brief courtship the two eloped, and were wed on August 26 that same year, in Campbell County, Kentucky, by Justice of the Peace James R Hallam. Although the marriage certificate states Dufour is the age of 18, she was only 14. Dufour was born in 1877, in Litchfield, Ohio. McCay places his age at 22.

Winsor McCay from the time of his birth, until the age of 18, 1867-1885, live in Spring Lake, Michigan.

The 1870 and 1880 Michigan censuses, which are the best records available indicating his birth year, both support the notion that Winsor McCay was born in 1867. That is, when you consider Gaines Madison Barney's method of recording age.

When this is revealed, there can be little doubt Winsor McCay was born in 1867.

The 1870 census conducted in Spring Lake on August 16, 1870, by Gaines M. Barney, documents "Zenis McKay" as being age 3, and born in Canada. Seeing the boy was less than six weeks away from his 3rd birthday, the number was rounded up.

A decade later, the 1880 census conducted in Spring Lake on June 2, 1880, by Dr. James O. Bates, documents "Zenas W. McKay" as being age 12, and born in Canada. Young McCay was nearly four months away from his next birthday, and Bates appears to have recorded exact ages at the time of the census, unlike Gaines M. Barney.

There has never been any dispute concerning the month and day of McCay's birth, September 26. That remained consistent throughout his life, and historians agree.

The year 1868 figures into Winsor McCay's August

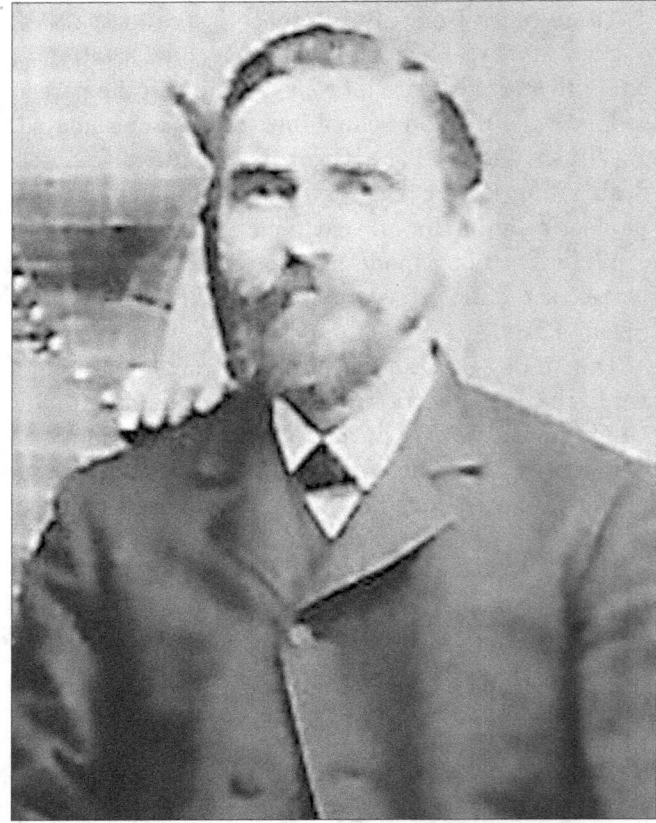

1870 Spring Lake census taker, Gaines M. Barney, the man behind all of the confusion.

26, 1891 marriage certificate when he wed Maude Dufour. McCay is listed at age 22. That would make his birthday September 26, 1868.

Winsor McCay's birthday is listed as September 26, 1869 in many resources and publications, and the headstone on his grave at Evergreens Cemetery in Brooklyn, New York reads 1869.

Another Winsor McCay published birthdate is September 26, 1871. It is a date Winsor McCay himself gave in an interview later in his life. This is false, because McCay appears in the 1870. McCay could not appear in a census one year *before* he was born.

Furthering the falsehood of McCay's 1871 birth date statement is that he said he was born in Spring Lake, Michigan. McCay was born in Canada. It's not a detail in dispute, even with Spring Lake historians, who would love more than anything to claim McCay was born in their hometown.

What is interesting is that the *Grand Haven Tribune*, the only Tri-Cities area newspaper in operation at the time of McCay's death in 1934, ran an Associated Press wire story that stated he was born September 26, 1871 in Spring Lake, Michigan.

Author John Canemaker points to an even earlier year for McCay's birth. He puts it at September 26, 1866. Canemaker bases this on the 1870 census, with McCay listed at age 3, at the moment it was conducted on August 16. McCay would have then turned age 4, six weeks later, on September 26. Thus, 1866 becomes his birth year.

However, Gaines M. Barney, who took the 1870 census in Spring Lake and dated and signed his name to it, had a numerical curve habit. He routinely rounded numbers up concerning the age of children. There is little exception to Barney's pattern in the 46 census pages he filled out from August 10-18th, 1870.

If a child had already celebrated his or her birthday prior to recording the census, Barney entered their age correctly. But if a child's next birthday was approaching within a couple of months, Barney rounded up their age up to the next number.

This can be verified through a comparison of surviving birth certificates other children have, which Winsor McCay does not.

Just as an example, we can look at the 1870 Spring Lake census in regards to the McCay family's known friends, Hunter Savidge and Aloys Bilz. Both had two children. Barney visited their homes, conducting the Spring Lake census 4 days earlier, on August 12.

Esther Savidge, born May 17, 1866, and Fanny Bilz, born May 7, 1867, are correctly recorded, at ages 4 and 3 respectively, as they had celebrated their birthdays shortly before the census was conducted.

William Savidge, born September 30, 1863, and Maggie Bilz, born October 25, 1868, are actually the ages of 6 and 1 at the taking of the census. However, Gaines M. Barney rounds up their ages to 7 and 2, even though William's birthday was 6 weeks away and Maggie's birthday was 11 weeks away.

Barney did the same thing with Winifred Walsh, daughter of Martin Walsh. Walsh was a close friend and associate of Winsor's father, Robert. Winifred Walsh, born October 20, 1860, was age 10 at the time the census was conducted at her home on August 13. Barney rounded Winifred's age up to 11 even though her birthday was nearly 10 weeks away.

Winsor Zenas McCay was actually age 2 when Barney stopped at the McCay residence on August 16, 1870. Seeing that Winsor was less than six weeks away from his next birthday on September 26, Bar-

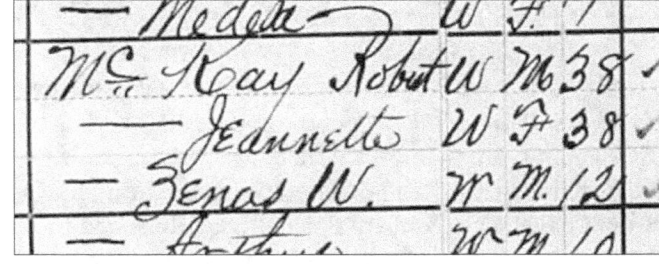

A snapshot of the 1870 Spring Lake census, conducted by Gaines M. Barney on August 16, 1870, at the McCay home. It notes "Zenis" (Winsor McCay) is the age of 3. McCay was actually 2. Barney rounded the number up to Winsor's approaching next birthday.

A snapshot of the 1880 Spring Lake census, conducted on June 2, 1880 notes "Zenas W." (Winsor McCay) is the age of 12.

ney rounded it up to age 3.

Thus, Winsor Zenas McCay was born September 26, 1867.

Being born in Canada, did Winsor McCay ever become a United States citizen? The answer is yes.

According to a naturalization law that included Canada, one only needed to be a resident of the United States for five years, after which time they automatically became a citizen. Robert McCay would have had to file a paper when he first arrived in America, noting intent to live here.

After that five year period Robert and Janet McCay became citizens, as did any foreign born children of the parents. So, Winsor McCay automatically became a citizen of the United States the day his parents did.

WINSOR McCAY'S NAMESAKE
The Man He Was Named For Who Influenced The Alpena Drawing

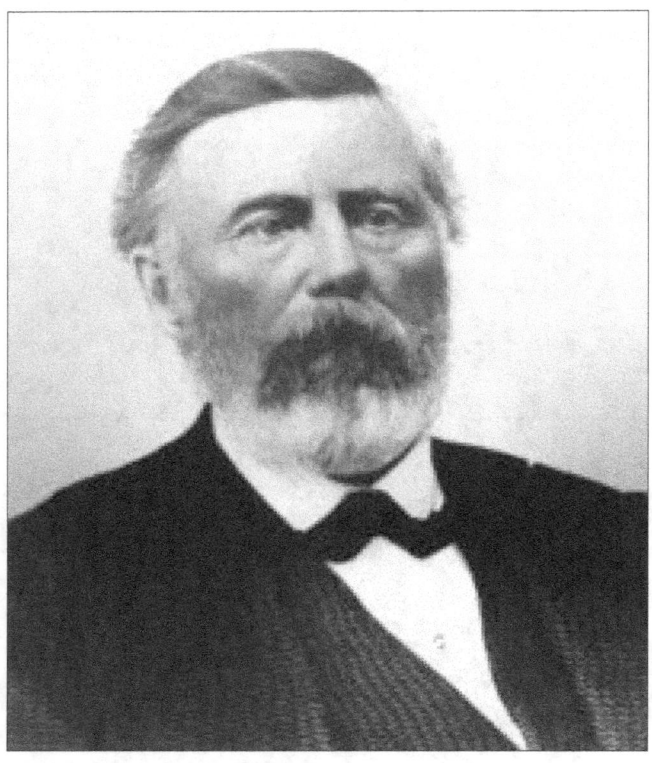

Zenas Gilbert Winsor, Winsor McCay's namesake.

Before the story of the Winsor McCay's illustration of *The Sinking of The Alpena* can be told, one has to learn about Zenas Gilbert Winsor.

If it wasn't for Zenas Gilbert Winsor, the McCays would have never come to Spring Lake. If it wasn't for him, artist Winsor Zenas McCay would have had another name. And if it wasn't for him, Winsor McCay's first "commercial illustration" likely wouldn't have been a drawing of the sinking passenger steamship named The Alpena.

Winsor McCay was born Zenas Winsor McKay.

By the time he was a teen, Zenas Winsor McKay was known by others primarily as Winsor Z. McKay. It wasn't until after the McKay family departed Spring Lake, Michigan, that Winsor's father, Robert McKay, changed the spelling of the family name to McCay.

Robert McCay was an employee of Zenas G. Winsor, who in some biographies is called "a great American entrepreneur." Much has been written in books concerning Zenas G. Winsor's enterprising exploits and his historical adventures in the state of Michigan. However, Zenas G. Winsor receives about one paragraph at best in books written about artist Winsor McCay.

Zenas G. Winsor and Robert McCay, the artist's father, met around 1862 in Ontario, Canada. Winsor, who resided in New York and traded stocks at the time, was establishing a business of trade involving the purchase and shipment of goods, from New York to his former hometown of Grand Rapids, Michigan.

Robert McCay, who resided in West Zorra Township, near Woodstock, in Ontario, Canada, took a job working for Mr. Winsor in that operation. During this period Robert McCay became familiar with Michigan, in particular, Kent and Ottawa Counties.

Robert McCay married Jeanette (Janet) Murray at the Methodist Episcopal Church in Woodstock, Canada, on January 8, 1866. Zenas G. Winsor encouraged McCay to move to Ottawa County, Michigan, where he was expanding his business, and also establishing a new one to serve the "Tri-Cities," representing Spring Lake, Grand Haven and Ferrysburg.

To bankroll the operation, Zenas G. Winsor had traveled to Enniskillen Township, Ontario, when a major oil deposit was discovered. Due to enormous prosperity a part of Enniskillen Township broke away, and the city of Petrolia was incorporated that year. Aware of the incredible financial opportunity, Zenas G. Winsor engaged in the operation of oil wells, and purchasing and selling oil at Petrolia. The endeavor proved moderately beneficial.

Zenas G. Winsor invested his earnings into the further development of his dry goods operation, and established the Winsor Coal, Salt & Cement Company, which formally opened an office in Grand Haven in 1868. He also expanded his forwarding, storage and commissioning business.

Robert McCay, newly wed, moved to Spring Lake with his wife Janet, where he worked as an unskilled teamster for Mr. Winsor, driving a horse team and wagon receiving and delivering orders for his employer's growing enterprise. But Zenas G. Winsor was not just Robert McCay's boss, they were also close friends.

Zenas G. Winsor assumed a mentorship role for 26-year-old Robert McCay. When Robert and Janet had their first child in 1867, they named the boy Zenas Winsor McCay. Robert hadn't just named his son after his employer, he had named his child after an important and deeply loved friend. Zenas G. Winsor's relation with his namesake would be akin to that of a grandfather.

Born Zenas Gilbert Winsor to Darius and Sally Winsor on December 14, 1814 in Skaneateles, Onondaga County, New York, Zenas grew up fast. He had to go to work at a young age to support his family in 1830, when his father was sentenced to prison, due to debts resulting from business misfortunes.

Thus, Zenas left school at the age 15, finding employment as a store clerk and then a physician's assistant. After his father was released from prison, Zenas came to Michigan in the spring of 1832, with his parents and six siblings, first settling in Ionia and then Grand Rapids.

In 1833, while working for the Grand River Transportation Company, Zenas G. Winsor was one of the first men to transport lumber up the river from Grand Rapids, and goods from Grand Haven to Ionia.

That same year he took a job as a clerk working for Rix Robinson, a pioneering fur trader. Winsor was in charge of the office at Grand Haven. His interaction with Native Americans earned him the Indian name "Chemokeemanee," which meant young Englishman.

In a published historical collection that detailed the early days of Ottawa County, Michigan, Zenas G. Winsor not only received recognition and praise for his contributions to the development of the area, but for his personality, as well:

He has not been a silent observer, but during all these years has contributed to the growth and improvement of the Grand River valley. For years he has been one of our leading business men and has commanded the respect and confidence of a large and growing community. Mr. Winsor is a gentleman of whom we all think well, and may he long remain among us.

Winsor wrote a paper on the early settlement of Ottawa County, Michigan, parts of which reveal what it was like for a young man in this area of the state at the time:

Ottawa, at that time, was a wilderness, without white inhabitants, save only an Indian mission at Grand Rapids with a Mr. Slater, wife, and one female teacher; an Indian trading post controlled by Louis Campau at Grand Rapids and Rix Robinson's trading posts at the mouth of the Thorn Apple and at Grand Haven.

Grand Haven being headquarters, has been made quite respectable in buildings. We had a store, warehouse with pole dock, and dwelling house with four rooms occupied by Mr. Robinson, and wife, who was a half-breed woman. Up to the fall of 1834, Grand Haven contained only Indians, and traders.

Spring Lake was the enterprise of the Whites, brothers-in-law of Mr. Ferry. So, on the other side of the river, Robinson [Township] was first entered by the Robinson family, who were in close connection, from the beginning, with the parties at the mouth of the Grand River.

Zenas G. Winsor was a hero of sorts to the residents of Ottawa County, not only for his righteous demeanor and community involvement, but also for his bravery. He once captured a criminal, which made local headlines.

When Anson Lyman, convicted of larceny in Grand Rapids on July 20, 1851, escaped the custody of a law officer escorting him to jail after sentencing, it was Zenas Winsor who apprehended the scoundrel a week later. But he didn't just capture Lyman, he arrested him. The story made the pages of the *Grand River Times*:

Z. G. Winsor, Esq., who rightly constituted himself as an officer and swore (although Zenas never swears) that the law, and its sentence should be duly executed upon the consummate and incorrigible thief.

It wasn't the first time Winsor made a citizen's arrest, but it was the most unusual criminal he apprehended. Lyman had stolen women's garments, including undergarments from a store, and while on the run was dressed like a woman when Winsor apprehended him and made a citizen's arrest.

The escapee, initially in irons, had freed himself of them with the aid of a friend, who was deemed an accomplice and apprehended later:

He had not got himself more than clear from the irons, with the aid of a friend, who we understand is already known, before Lyman commenced his business with stealing shirts, and we were about to write that other word, but modesty forbids, boots and shoes, watches, knives, and anything he could lift. Judge [Israel V.] Harris will not hesitate to send him up for five or seven and a day.

Winsor spent two years prospecting for gold in California with an associate. His experience in Sacramento City, California during a historic flood was anything but pleasant, as indicated in a March 9, 1852 piece written by Winsor's partner, and published in the *Grand Rapids Inquirer*:

On Saturday the 6th, the levee on the American River broke away, and the water came rushing into the upper end of the town in torrents. Mr. Z. G. Winsor and myself are keeping a hay yard for the purpose of selling hay and keeping animals. On Sunday morning the water came rushing down through our yard. We had to get a boat, the water being four feet deep.

In 1849, while living in Kent County, Michigan, Winsor got behind a petition to procure a fire engine. This led to the development of the Grand Rapids Fire Department.

Winsor also dealt in livestock, and in September 1859 won recognition for cows and bulls he bred, at the 11th annual Kent County Agricultural Society event, in Grand Rapids, Michigan.

Zenas Winsor was married three times during his life. His first marriage, in 1838 to Emily Hopkins, lasted eight months, ending when she died unexpectedly. The Hopkins family, whose ancestry included the famous Revolutionary War hero Ethan Allen, was well-known and respected in Ottawa County. Winsor remarried, taking Hannah Tower as his second wife on August 2, 1840. After she died in 1869, he married again, exchanging vows with Anne Kilgore in 1874.

In the book, *A History of Grand Rapids*, the entry on Zenas G. Winsor spoke of his ambition and kindness:

Mr. Winsor has always been a busy man. He could never be idle. He would always be doing something, either on his own account, or for somebody else, wide awake and ready to push things. Of temperate and regular habits, socially he is genial and pleasant and uniformly friendly; a gentleman enjoying good will and good wishes for everybody in this community.

In 1863, Winsor sold the dry goods business he had operated for three years and traveled to Nevada, where he had a large investment in silver mines. But he remained there only three months after discovering his investment of $30,000 (the equivalent of over $570,000 today), was irrevocably lost.

The financial hit opened Winsor's eyes to any opportunity that could produce a quick return. The average man would have faced irreversible ruin, but not Zenas Gilbert Winsor. He journeyed back to his native New York, where he operated moderately in stocks and engaged in the purchasing and shipping of goods to Grand Rapids.

Then in 1866, Winsor saw an incredible opportunity in Petrolia, Ontario, Canada, where oil had been found. He packed up and headed there, engaging in the petroleum trade, but enjoyed only a moderate profit.

It's no wonder that biographies published about Zenas G. Winsor call him "a great American Entrepreneur."

In 1866, Winsor began developing a forwarding, storage and commissioning business in Ottawa County, Michigan. He also established the groundwork for the Winsor Coal, Salt & Cement Company, into which he brought Robert McCay as an employee.

The company was a wholesale and retail dealer in anthracite and bituminous coals, Eastern and Saginaw (coarse, fine and dairy) salt, land and calcined plaster, Cheboygan and Milwaukee quick lime, Portland, Akron and Oswego cement, plastering hair, and fire brick and fire clay. Land plaster was a specialty sold in barrels, bags and bulk.

The coal, salt, and cement enterprise was formally designated by 1868, and continued operation until about 1885, when Zenas G. Winsor moved back to Grand Rapids to live.

Now, we can get to the McCays taking up residence in Spring Lake, and young Winsor McCay's pathway to drawing his first commercial illustration on the blackboard of his classroom in 1880, *The Sinking of The Alpena*.

WINSOR McCAY'S BOYHOOD
His Interest In Art And Influences Growing Up In Spring Lake

Winsor Zenas McCay's father, Robert McCay, was born in 1840 in West Zorra, Ontario, Canada. The third of six children born to Donald and Christiana McCay, Robert married neighbor Jeanette (Janet) Murray on January 8, 1866 at the Methodist Episcopal Church, in Woodstock, Canada. Janet, born 1841 in East Zorra, was the daughter of Peter and Mary Murray.

As previously mentioned, Zenas G. Winsor, whom Robert had met and worked with a few years earlier, encouraged McCay to move to Ottawa County, Michigan, where he was expanding one business, while establishing a new one trading in coal, salt and cement. With guaranteed employment, Robert and Janet McCay came to Michigan in 1866 assuming residency in Spring Lake, Ottawa County.

Robert McCay had crossed the Ontario border into Michigan previously (in 1862) after he had met, and earlier employed by, Zenas G. Winsor.

Robert McCay first worked as an unskilled teamster, driving a horse-led wagon during the establishment of Zenas G. Winsor's Coal, Salt & Cement Company.

The McCays resided in a rental home during their first four years in Spring Lake.

In September 1867, Janet McCay returned to West Zorra, Ontario to be with her family for the birth of their first child, a son, born on September 26, 1867. It appears Robert McCay named his son after his employer, a man he greatly admired, Zenas Winsor. Thus, Zenas Winsor McCay entered the world.

Robert and Janet McCay would have two more children, Arthur who was born in 1869, and Mae (Mary), born in 1876.

During his childhood growing up in Spring Lake, Winsor McCay developed his imagination and creativity drawing pictures of everyday surroundings. And there was a lot surrounding him to draw, from sawmills, to trains, to ships.

In 1870, Robert McCay had saved enough money to purchase a parcel of land from Aloys Bilz. McCay bought the southern half of lot 5, block 3, on the corner of Meridian and Tolford Streets, for $150. On that land was built the McCay home.

The Tolford Street location was ideal, as it was only one block away from Spring Lake Union School, on East Exchange Street, where the McCay children would attend school. It was also only two blocks away from the main thoroughfare, Savidge Street, where many retail businesses were located.

Aloys Bilz and his family became close friends of the McCay family. Aside from being a realtor, Bilz was a retail business owner. His business, located on Savidge Street, sold hardware, building materials, tin ware, steam fittings, plumbing supplies, furniture, stoves and appliances of the day.

So Bilz didn't just sell someone a parcel of land on which to build a house, he also provided the materials

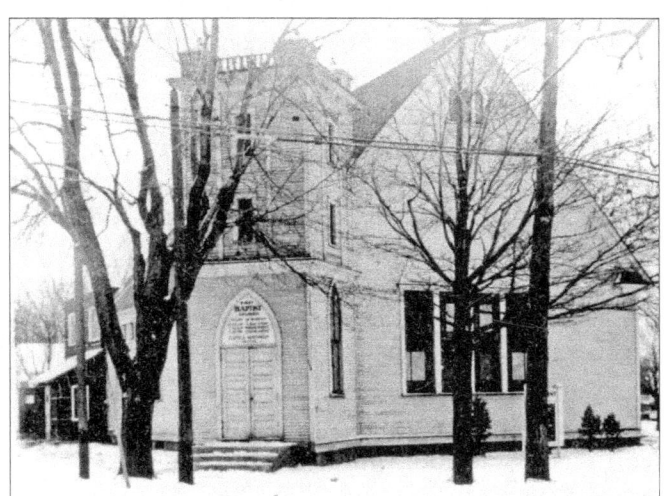
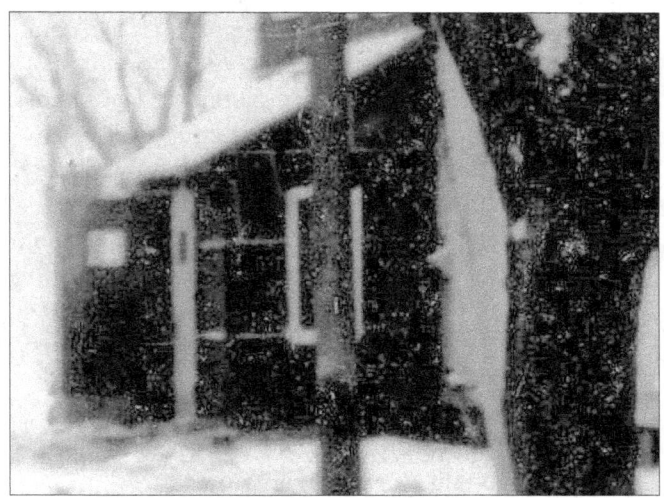

The only existing photograph that provides a glimpse of the McCay home on a snowy day in Spring Lake, Michigan. At left, behind the pole in back of the First Baptist Church, is a glimpse of a portion of the McCay house on the corner of Meridian and Tolford Streets. At right, an enlargement of the visible portion of the home lacks detail, but you can see someone has left a door open to an entryway.

to build your home and furnish it, too.

But the new McCay house didn't stand for long. Tragically, on October 8, 1871, a massive fire broke out in Spring Lake that wasn't brought under control until the following day. While no lives were lost in the blaze, one casualty was the McCay home. It was destroyed in the blaze.

The fire destroyed much of Spring Lake Village and left 70 families homeless. Newspaper reports and records show that Aloys Bilz was the hardest hit and suffered the greatest financial loss. He lost his business, home, and many of his properties. He was able to rebuild his home and business thanks to a $30,000 loan extended by friend, Hunter Savidge. Savidge, a prominent and wealthy lumberman.

Robert, Janet and their two sons, Winsor and Arthur, had to reside elsewhere for a short period. Their second home was rebuilt on the same parcel of land, at the corner of Meridian and Tolford Streets.

The fire started in the Haire & Tolford Sawmill, which was located on the Grand River, near the foot of Division Street, two blocks west of the McCay home. Reports pointed to embers being emitted from a vessel's smokestack moored at the mill's dock as the cause.

Miraculously, The First Baptist Church, which stood two doors north of the McCay home, on the corner of Meridian and Exchange Streets, survived the fire, due to the efforts of members of the congregation.

An account of the tragic fire was published in an Ottawa County historical publication:

On the 8th of October, 1871, the church bells sounded the alarm of fire. By night all were out fighting the fire. Churches were closed, clergy and people fought the fire demon's power side by side. People escaped with their lives from the fierce heat, the blinding smoke and the tempest of wind.

The loss of the McCay home yielded family folklore concerning Winsor McCay's "first" illustration.

John Canemaker reveals the story in his book, *Winsor McCay: His Life and Art*, and how it established young Winsor's ability to remove himself emotionally from an event, to create a descriptive picture. A tale told within the McCay family for years, described four-year-old Winsor etching a drawing on a frosted glass pane, after fire had destroyed his home "one freezing night." Canemaker wrote:

The family was rescued and sheltered at a neighbor's home, where Winsor picked up a five penny nail, which was lying on the windowsill, and unthinkingly commenced to etch the catastrophe on the frosted window pane.

Winsor's mother, Janet, later in life, told a relative a story that became part of the family folklore. She relayed her son, Winsor, at the age of six, could draw beautifully. Thus Winsor began drawing at age four, but was doing a beautiful job of it by age six.

It was very cold the evening the McCay home burned down. Fruit growers in Ottawa County were well aware of early "killing frosts," and watchful of how daytime temperatures could plunge, from a last breath of summer, to a whisper of winter, overnight.

The effect the fire had on Robert McCay and his family was in one sense a tragedy, and in another, an example of community love and outreach. The scale of the fire in Spring Lake quickly turned acquaintances into close friends.

Perhaps no one but Aloys Bilz had more of an influence on Robert McCay during his early years in Spring Lake. Granted, Zenas G. Winsor played an enormous role in Robert McCay's life in the area, but their relationship developed into more of a "father" role for Robert, and "Grandpa," or godfather, to the McCay children.

Bilz inspired Robert to imagine developing a career in real estate, which McCay did pursue after leaving the area in 1885.

It's possible the McCays moved into their second home as early as Thanksgiving Day, 1871. It was reported that neighbors who hadn't lost their homes pitched in as volunteers, to assist in construction for those who did, speeding up the process.

In the fall of 1872, Winsor McCay reached the age of five. Where he would attend school wasn't a choice. Spring Lake Union School was a block away from the McCay home.

Union School, constructed in 1869, was a "graded school," meaning that it conducted classes for all grades, from elementary to high school level, all under one roof.

According to grammar school age requirements, Winsor McCay began attending Spring Lake Union School, in the fall of 1872 or early 1873. There were as many as five instructors at the school at that time.

The school grew as Winsor grew up. In 1873, a north wing was added to the school. An upper floor was completed and furnished in 1880, expanding the structure to eight rooms total.

The year Winsor McCay began attending the

school, students in attendance numbered nearly 200.

Those in authority in Spring Lake took education seriously. Parents allowing children to be truant were held accountable.

While Winsor McCay would play hooky on occasion from school, the legendary notion that he was notoriously truant, or barely attended school, is untrue. His father was on the school board. Winsor graduated from Union School, perhaps not with honors, but according to records, met all requirements.

About the time Winsor McCay began attending Union School, his father Robert became friends with Martin Walsh, a grape-grower who owned a grocery store. Walsh had assisted in framing the Spring Lake Village charter and was one of the community's earliest Presidents.

Walsh, Bilz and McCay became political allies and Robert McCay and his buddies appeared on Spring Lake ballots, seeking office.

Robert McCay became outspoken on the dangers of fires, most of which originated from sawmills along the Grand River and the railway and sawmills near the shoreline of Spring Lake.

Union School was a busy place, but young Winsor McCay stood out recognized for his artistic creativity. From an early age, McCay had an interest in navigation, and considering his surroundings, this was not unusual. A two minute walk south from the McCay home placed you on the bank of the Grand River. A five minute walk north from the McCay home brought you to the shore of Spring Lake.

The Grand River bustled with schooners, steamers, tugboats, sailboats and barges. Most were involved in the receipt and transport of lumber and goods. Spring Lake teemed with similar vessels, also boats that were suited for, and used for, recreational purposes.

The lake, Spring Lake, was where Winsor McCay and his classmates Henry Root and Hubert Hicks would have gone to fish and swim. The big event every summer in Spring Lake was of the Regatta, which attracted thousands of tourists and skilled competitors who engaged in sailboat races.

In 1875, Winsor's namesake, Zenas G. Winsor, took the position of agent for the Goodrich Transpor-

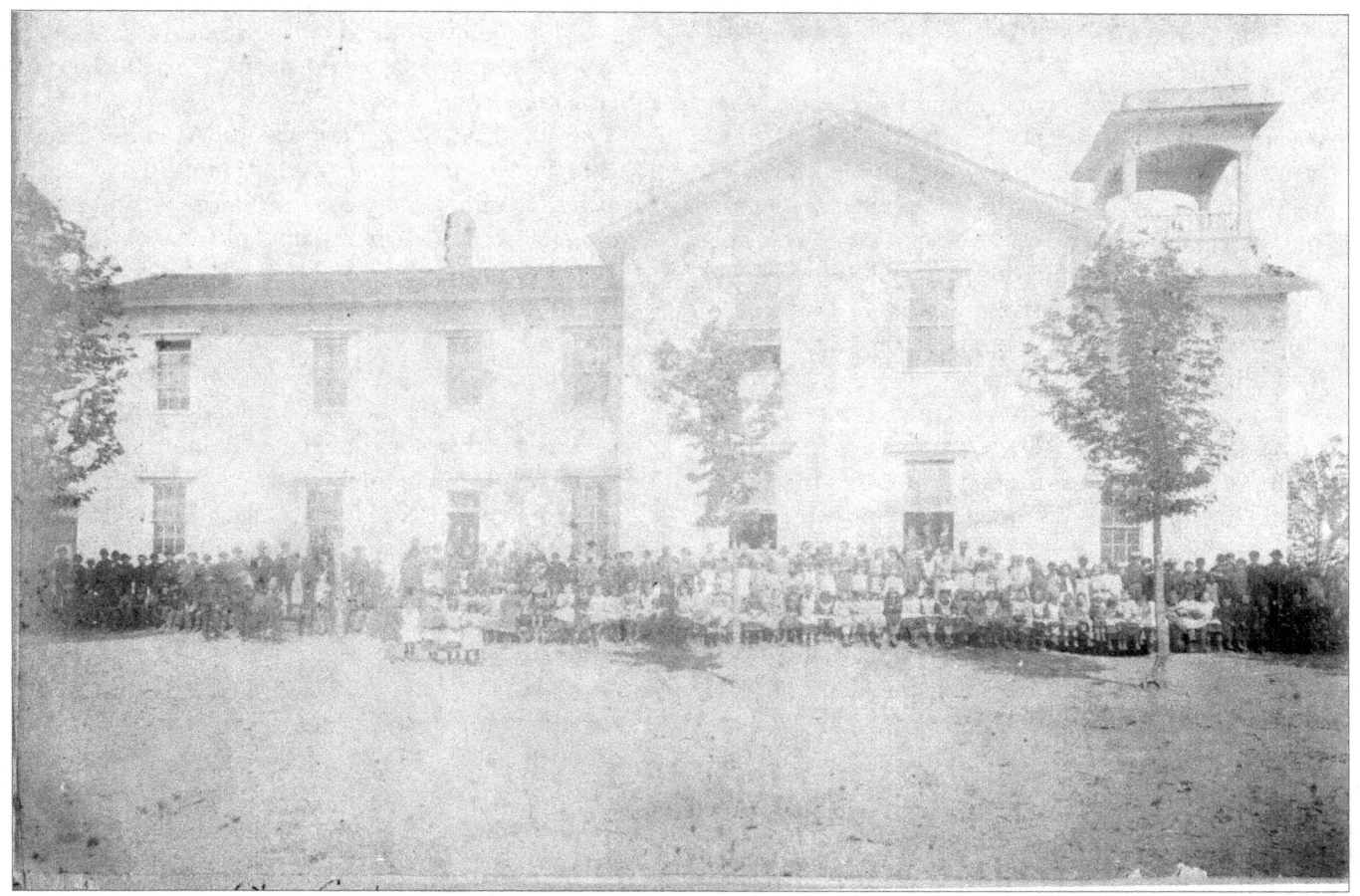

The two-story Spring Lake Union School, as it looked in 1880, the year Winsor McCay drew his *The Sinking of The Alpena* illustration on his classroom blackboard.

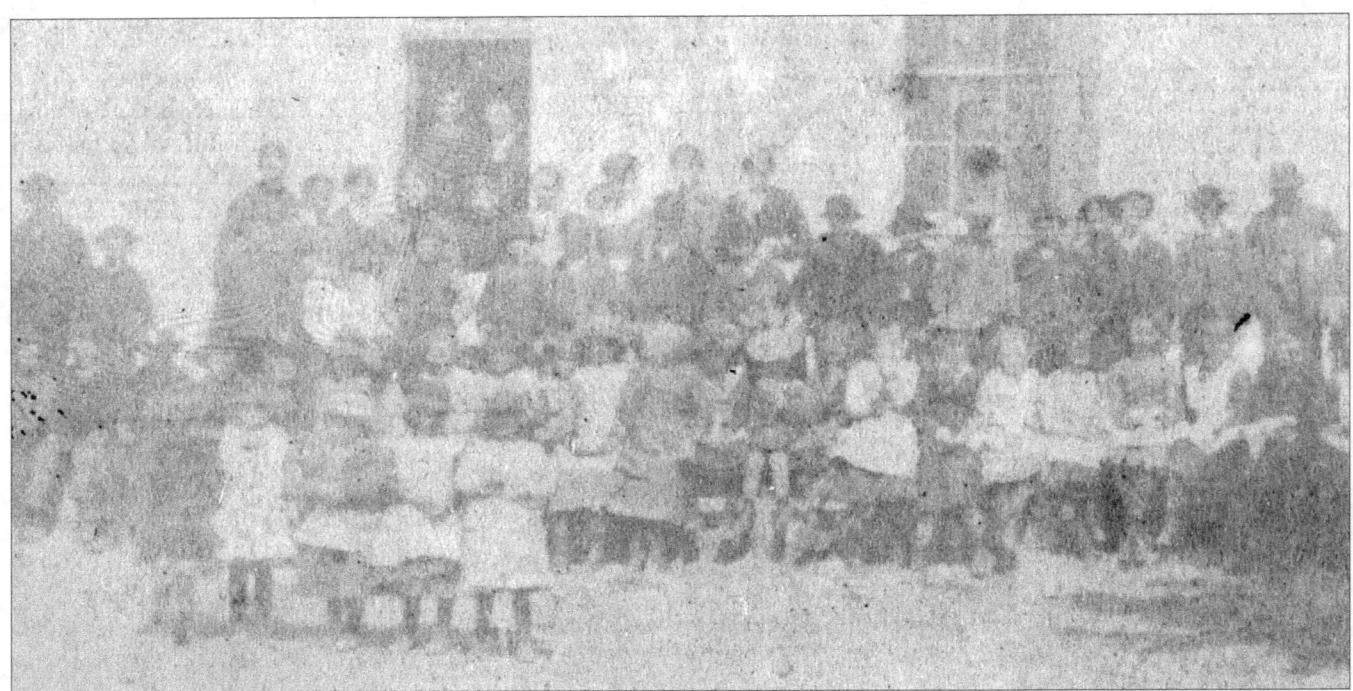

Students posing for the 1880 photo. Is Winsor McCay among the crowd? That remains undetermined.

tation Company, which operated passenger ships out of the neighboring Grand Haven port. The port was situated on the Grand River, which opened up to Lake Michigan.

Robert McCay, like so many others in Spring Lake, routinely traveled over the Grand River bridge, into Grand Haven, to conduct business. His job also demanded it, as Zenas G. Winsor's Coal, Salt & Cement Company maintained its warehouse in the city.

At times, Robert would take his sons, Winsor and Arthur, along on these trips to Grand Haven, and drop them off at the port to enjoy the sights under the watchful eyes of Zenas G. Winsor.

As an agent for the Goodrich Transportation Company, Mr. Winsor was in charge of selling every ticket and booking every passenger aboard a Goodrich passenger ship. His office occupied a prominent place at the port.

All types of vessels, such as schooners and large cargo ships packed with goods, arrived and departed from the port daily. Numerous passenger ships with routes to and from Chicago, Milwaukee, and Kenosha, also embarked and disembarked daily. Steamers tied up at the docks between arrival and departure could easily be toured with Goodrich agent Zenas G. Winsor as your guide.

Winsor McCay wrote of his youth and interest in artwork later in life, offering a glimpse of his childhood in Spring Lake. The memoir appeared in John Canemaker's McCay book:

"I just couldn't stop drawing, anything and everything. I did not do this to amuse someone else, or to show off how good I could draw. I drew alone to please myself.

I never cared at all if anyone else liked my drawings, nor did I get discouraged if I made a bad one. I never saved my drawings. I would give them away if anyone wanted them or would throw them away.

I drew on fences, blackboards in school, old scraps of paper, slates, sides of barns—I just couldn't stop."

The largest wooden "fence" canvas near his boyhood residence was the "The Pound," located only one block northwest of the McCay home.

The Pound was an uncovered area enclosed by a 16-foot wooden fence. It was a place where escaped farm animals were kept until their owners claimed them. McCay family friend Martin Walsh, an Ottawa County resident, best described it in a published memoir:

"In those days the office of Pound master was so important that the best men in town were usually elected and accepted the office. Young boys were always on the lookout for escaped hogs, and even went as far as letting them out of the pens on purpose, in order to obtain the monetary reward offered by the Pound master."

It was an active and popular place for neighborhood children to hang out, including for young Winsor McCay, who certainly brought along a piece of chalk, a pencil, or paint and a small brush.

According to John Canemaker's book on McCay, Winsor's mother Janet once told a relative that Winsor got in trouble for drawing in school books.

Janet said her son used to get whipped in school, by teachers, for drawing pictures in the margins of his classroom textbooks. She conveyed that Winsor was always drawing pictures at school, and that it was of little use for teachers to punish the boy as "nothing could stop him."

There are two things Winsor McCay historians would agree on concerning his adult professional art career. One: The most famous comic strip character he created was *Little Nemo*. Two: People, places and things McCay was exposed to in his personal life routinely made their way into his creations and his illustrations.

The *Little Nemo in Slumberland* comic ran in newspapers from 1905 to 1914, and 1924 to 1926. Little Nemo was also the star of McCay's pioneering 1911 animated film cartoon, *Winsor McCay, the Famous Cartoonist of the N.Y. Herald and His Moving Comics* (also known as *Little Nemo*). It was the very first film cartoon produced in the United States.

Little Nemo's fantastic adventures took place in bed, asleep, in his dreams. The adventure ended when he awoke in the last panel of each comic strip. Thus, Nemo, left his bedroom to venture to far off places.

Could a Spring Lake boy named Robbie Patterson have been an influence in the creation of Little Nemo?

It is known that Winsor McCay modeled the likeness of Little Nemo after his young son, Robert. However, the gimmick of a fantasy dream world came from his imagination, not from his son. And McCay's imagination was fueled by things he had experienced, or been exposed to.

So who was Robbie Patterson and what happened?

Robert (Robbie) Patterson, born 1860 in Ramsay, Ontario, Canada, was the oldest of David and Catherine Patterson's three children. His father, an affluent, well-liked prominent lumberman, owned Patterson & Company, a mill across from the D&M depot at Spring Lake.

Robbie, seven years older than Winsor McCay (who was nearly eight at the time) also attended Spring Lake Union School. While the two likely didn't share a mutual classroom, certainly interacted and knew each other.

On the night of July 11, 1875, a neighbor saw what he believed was a prowler atop Patterson's two-story home. However, on closer examination, it was Robbie, fast asleep, walking on the roof. The lad was in slumber land, completely unaware of his adventure. He had climbed out of his second-story bedroom window, scaled a lighting rod to the top of the home and was enjoying a stroll on the roof.

Witnesses were afraid to awake the child for fear he would fall. After about an hour, Robbie climbed down the steeple, went through his second-story bedroom window, then crawled back into bed. When he was awakened, he knew nothing of his adventure and only learned of it from those who witnessed it.

An article about Robbie's precarious sleepwalking exploit appeared in the *Spring Lake Independent*, a weekly newspaper published by John G. Lee and David R. Waters. The story, published on July 16, 1875,

A Somnambulist's Capers.

On the night of the 11th a strange case of somnambulism occurred at Spring Lake, Mich., the principal actor being a lad named Robbie, son of David Patterson, a prominent lumberman. At about 1 A. M., a neighbor hearing a noise, and fearing burglars, arose, and looking out of the window saw what he supposed to be a man climbing the lightning rod of Patterson's residence. He immediately gave the alarm, when it was noticed that the object made no attempt to escape, and acted strangely. Curiosity being aroused, his movements were very closely watched. The boy climbed to the highest point of the Gothic tower, and, although the surface was very uneven, explored the whole top of the building without a misstep. After remaining upon the roof for nearly an hour, he returned to the rod, climbed down to the second story, and getting into the window of his own room, went to bed, where he was found sound asleep soon after. Upon being awakened, he remembered nothing of his strange trip, and was very much frightened when told where he had been. Next day he was much exhausted and quite sick.

Article detailing the exploits of the sleepwalking Spring Lake youth Robbie Patterson, originally published in *The Spring Lake Independent*, republished in *The Grand Advance*, July 20, 1875.

was picked up and reprinted nationally in newspapers across the country later that month, under the headline: *A Somnambulist's Capers*. The entire article reads as follows:

On the night of the 11th of July a strange case of somnambulism occurred at Spring Lake, Michigan, the principal actor being a lad named Robbie, the son of David Patterson, a prominent lumberman.

At about 1 a.m., a neighbor hearing a noise, and fearing burglars, arose, and looking out of the window saw what he supposed to be a man climbing the lightning rod of Patterson's residence. He immediately gave the alarm, when it was noticed the object made no attempt to escape, and acted strangely. Curiosity being aroused, his movements were closely watched.

The boy climbed to the highest point of the Gothic tower, and although the surface was very uneven, explored the whole top of the building without a misstep.

After remaining upon the roof for nearly an hour, he returned to the rod, climbed down to the second story, and getting into the window of his own room, went to bed, where he was found asleep soon after.

Upon being awakened, he remembered nothing of the strange trip, and was very much frightened when told where he had been. The next day he was much exhausted and quite sick.

Dozens of newspapers from coast to coast reprinted the *Spring Lake Independent* article. The talk of the town expanded to become the talk of a nation. Robbie Patterson's odd adventure literally put Spring Lake on the national map in 1875.

The Grange Advance (Red Wing, Minnesota), *The Weekly Register* (Point Pleasant, West Virginia), *The Weekly Caucasian* (Lexington, Missouri) were only a few examples. Michigan newspapers reprinting the work included *The Lake County Star* in Chase, among others.

With the passing of his wife Catherine, Robbie's father moved his family to the city of White Cloud, in Newaygo, Michigan, before 1880.

The question is: Did Winsor McCay's *Little Nemo in Slumberland* comic strip originate from a childhood neighbor's nighttime sleepwalking adventure? Only Winsor McCay himself could tell us that if he were still alive, as the tale such as this never passed into family folklore.

But this we do know: Winsor McCay as an artist was influenced by sights and experiences encountered in his environment. As mentioned, images from carnival sideshows influenced his art depictions and design. There are many other such examples of influence that popped up in his illustrations.

Did Robbie Patterson alone foster the idea for Little Nemo? Likely not. Was Robbie Patterson's sleeping exploit at very least a small component in the creation of Little Nemo? Sure, why not?

It's much harder to believe to two are completely unrelated and merely a coincidence.

According to John Canemaker's book, once Winsor saw something, he examined it closely, and photographically remembered the most intricate details when creating an illustration of the subject.

Winsor's mother said that her talented son drew with incredible detail beginning at a very early age.

Living near mills, Winsor McCay frequently saw lumber being transported by ship and wagon. One winter, he illustrated a sleigh loaded with logs. He depicted every bolt head in the correct place on the side of the transport. Janet McCay relayed that her son even included the owner's markings on the ends of the logs.

While Winsor stated that he didn't care if others liked what he drew, that was all about to change in October 1880. Using his photographic memory of a passenger steamer at the Grand Haven port that he toured, and saw up close and personal with Zenas G. Winsor as his guide, Winsor would illustrate a historic and tragic moment on the blackboard of his classroom at Union School.

This moment in McCay's life greatly influenced an animation film short he would illustrate and produce 38 years later, titled *The Sinking of the Lusitania*.

Winsor McCay's real life Lusitania was a passenger ship named the Alpena. On October 15, 1880, the steamer broke apart during a violent storm and sank with all 80 souls aboard.

The man young Winsor McCay was named after, Zenas G Winsor, while not responsible for the disaster, was suddenly cast into the limelight due to the tragedy. It was a game-changer for Winsor McCay.

He would discover at the age of 13 that his hobby of drawing pictures could actually earn money, much to his father's disapproval. Robert McCay wanted his son to secure a business degree.

With the illustration of *The Sinking of The Alpena* came the moment the young illustrator imagined that a career in art no longer seemed like a dream, but a real possibility.

"THE SINKING OF THE ALPENA"
The Story Behind Winsor McCay's First Commercial Illustration

Friday, October 15, 1880 had been a beautiful day, described as "Indian summer-like." The sun went down as the passenger ship Alpena sat docked at the Grand Haven port.

Zenas G. Winsor sold the last tickets and booked the final passengers aboard the ship. Lamp lit docks illuminated a patiently waiting crowd as the call went out, "All aboard." Nearly eighty people of all ages boarded the ship and the Alpena departed the port at 9:30 P.M. Her destination: Chicago, Illinois.

The Alpena, a side-wheeled steamer built in 1866, by Thomas Arnold of Gallagher & Company (Marine City, Michigan), stretched a length of 197 feet, with a 26.66 foot beam, and a depth of 12 feet. The weight of the vessel was rated at 654 tons.

The Goodrich Transportation Company purchased the ship in April 1868. The vessel had undergone a renovation with upgrades in 1875, the same year Zenas G. Winsor became an agent for the company, operating the office at the Grand Haven port.

The wood-hulled steamer was powered by a single cylinder, vertical beam engine, which drove a pair of 24' radius side wheels. It was distinctive due to the "walking beam" engine, which was plainly visible above the massive side wheels. It had a forward pilothouse, strengthening arches along each side and a single smokestack.

While the day had been "summer-like," barometric pressure readings indicated an impending storm. Warnings had been transmitted via telegraph, warning of potentially hazardous conditions developing on Lake Michigan.

Zenas G. Winsor was aware of this, as he had received the telegram. But releasing the Alpena for departure was the company's decision, not that of Winsor. Thus, even with a storm looming, Goodrich allowed the ship to embark on her journey.

The steamship The Muskegon, spotted the Alpena in the distance on Lake Michigan, as waves began to kick up at 1:00 A.M., but reported that "everything seemed normal."

At about 3:00 A.M. in the early hours of October 16, what was later reported to be "the worst gale in Lake Michigan recorded history" swept across the water.

Captain George Boomsluiter of the barge The City

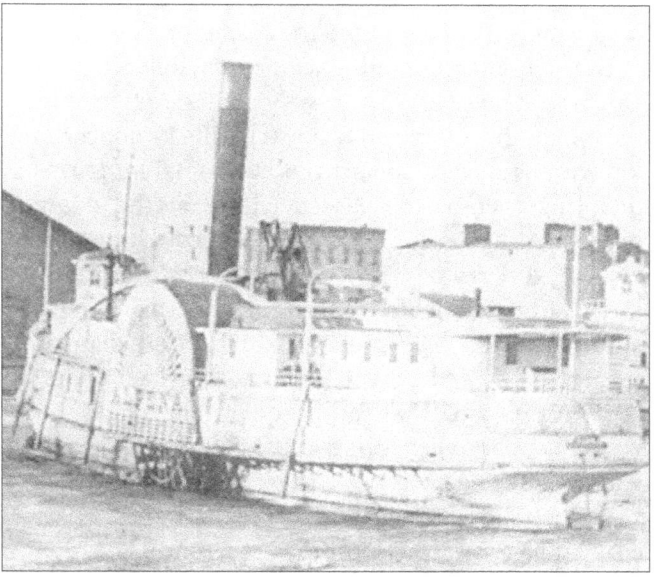

An early photo of the passenger steamer The Alpena, before her lower portion was painted black.

of Grand Haven, witnessed the Alpena in the distance, laboring in heavy and high waves about 35 miles off the shore of Kenosha, Wisconsin from 6:00 to 8:00 A.M. that morning.

Shortly thereafter, the Alpena broke apart, battered by large waves.

Several other ship captains kept a navigational spyglass on the vessel over the next several hours. One reported seeing the Alpena at a distance lying on her side with one of her paddle-wheels out of the water.

Ten car loads of apples were secured on her main deck, and some later speculated that the cargo had become unmanageable in the storm, and shifted, leading to the Alpena capsizing.

The wind calmed and currents shifted, marking the end of a storm that earned the name "The Big Blow" in Michigan writings.

But the suspense had only just begun for the Alpena, as her whereabouts were unknown.

At first, newspapers only reported that the ship was missing, and there existed a fear that she had gone down in the storm. That fear grew when the first reports of discovered debris appeared on October 18. This report was published in a Chicago paper:

Chicago, October 18 – The fate of the Alpena is still in doubt. The only information, in addition to the Associated Press, is obtained from dispatches and facts in possession of the Goodrich line here. It is learned that two vessels sighted the vessel thirty to fifty miles off Racine, Wisconsin Saturday afternoon, and another picked up a step ladder and pail marked "Alpena" at Holland, Michigan. A tug has been sent on a general lookout along the Michigan coast.

But debris kept coming ashore at Holland, Michigan, and Zenas G. Winsor was documenting communications from friends and families concerning known passengers aboard the missing ship. It was a daunting task, as the passenger log for the steamer had ended up on the ship, and Winsor didn't have a copy to work from.

The first published reports of the Alpena having sunk appeared on October 19, when unmistakable evidence surfaced that the ship had broken apart. A report went out that a portion of the ship's deck washed ashore near Montague, Michigan. Bodies began washing ashore, too, the first recovered being that of Mrs. Newton Bradley, of Santa Fe, New Mexico. She had spent the summer at Grand Haven with two of her children, Allie, age 25, and Kate, age 16. All three perished in the shipwreck. Now there was little doubt that no survivors would be found.

On October 23, the *Holland City News* described the total devastation in a published article:

The wreck is complete. She is broken into small fragments. The stern part of her hull lies near the harbor. The whole coast for 20 miles is strewn with the debris, freight, etc. The largest piece to land near Holland was the piano, it being barely able to float, our sailors concluded that she did not come very far. And the arrival of other heavy pieces of the wreck would seem to corroborate this.

Other Michigan newspapers reported shingles, lath, lumber and other pieces of the ship covered about 20 miles of Michigan shoreline. It also was reported that thousands of apples were found bobbing in the surf at Saugatuck.

By Tuesday, October 19, the harsh reality concerning the fate of the Alpena gripped the citizens of Ottawa County. The steamer had not pulled into a port somewhere seeking shelter. There had been no rescue boats dispatched when she broke apart. The general public understood that hope of seeing any survivors was over.

While no passengers aboard the ship were from Spring Lake, the McCays knew some of the individuals who had perished from neighboring Grand Haven.

The deceased citizens of Grand Haven included the

THE GREAT STORM.

A Gale With a Velocity of 48 Miles per Hour.

The Steamer Alpena Lost With 80 Lives.

Headline published in the Spring Lake newspaper *The Republican*, days after the disaster.

vessel's First Engineer, Robert W. Johnson, and Second Engineer, Robert Patton. Passengers from the city included Whitman S. Benham, editor of the *Grand Haven Herald* newspaper, and his wife, Sarah Benham, Montgomery Crossman, who was a foreman at Stearns Manufacturing Company, Heber Squier Jr., and Mary Curtis. Also of Ottawa County was Elijah Angel, from Lamont.

Winsor McCay was personally affected by the tragedy, much like the fire that took the McCay home 9 years earlier. His namesake, Zenas G. Winsor, the man who was like a grandfather to him and had given him a tour of the Alpena at the Grand Haven port, was now in an incredible state of anguish.

Zenas G. Winsor had sold every ticket and booked every passenger aboard the Alpena—all of whom were now dead. He was in charge of contacting the families of the deceased to inform them their loved ones were not coming home.

To make matters worse Lake Michigan was giving up few bodies. And the recovery was slow as bodies washed ashore for several weeks. Zenas G. Winsor was in charge of notifying families when a body of a loved one was recovered, to make arrangements as to where to send the remains.

Many newspapers included in their Alpena shipwreck coverage details of the recovery effort regarding human remains. This included publication of telegrams sent regarding recovered bodies of passengers, all of which were transmitted and signed by Zenas G. Winsor.

One such example was an article published in the October 22 edition of the *Oconto County Reporter*, of Green Bay, Wisconsin, which included a telegram sent by Zenas G. Winsor to the Mayor of Oconto:

Headline: The Wind's Wreck

The storm of Friday night and Saturday of last week was the worst experienced on the lakes for years. Many a noble vessel went down during the terrible gale, and many persons were hurried to eternity by the angry waters. From all directions reports of disasters come in thick and fast, while the death list keeps increasing with fearful rapidity. But the saddest of all is the loss of the Goodrich steamer Alpena, which went down on Lake Michigan with all on board—over one hundred persons in all. So far as is known, not a soul is left to tell the tale. When the news reached this city considerable anxiety was felt for the safety of Mrs. McConnell of this city, stewardess on the ill-fated steamer. The slender thread on which their hopes hung was broken on Thursday forenoon when the following telegram was received:

GRAND HAVEN, Mich., Oct. 21, 1880 - MAYOR OF OCONTO:

Tell Mrs. Lamkey we think we had the body of Mrs. McConnell.

What disposition shall we make of the body?

Z. G. WINSOR

According to the statement of the Goodrich folks at Chicago, Mrs. McConnell left the boat some ten days ago, and they do not think that she was on board. But her trunk has been washed ashore, and there is scarcely a doubt but that she has met a watery grave. Her nephew, John Lamkey, left for Grand Haven, Thursday night, to take charge of the body if found.

Five bodies, at last advices, had been washed ashore. The beach for miles near Holland, Michigan, is strewn with the debris of the ill-fated craft.

The October 23, 1880 edition of Spring Lake's The Republican newspaper reported the sinking of the Alpena topped with the headlines: "The Great Storm" and "The Steamer Alpena Lost With 80 Lives." Publisher Aloys Bilz provided national news mixed with local reporting.

The Republican provided for Spring Lake readers the sad course of events:

The elements and all else seemed calm here on Friday last week, October 15, and when the steamers and a number of vessels left our harbor in the evening all casual observers predicted a pleasant night, but appearances were ever deceiving, they were then.

The numerous wrecks all over the lake which space forbids us from noticing at length this week, testify to

Portion of an article published in the Spring Lake newspaper *The Republican*, days after the disaster, questioning whether the steamer was seaworthy and should have departed port with knowledge of the impending storm.

the fearful night which followed, such a night that was probably never known on the tempestuous waters of Lake Michigan.

The Republican interviewed several area seniors about the storm, noted bodies coming ashore with biographies of the deceased and hinted the Alpena as being unseaworthy:

The oldest inhabitants never knew the winds to blow so hard. Six bodies of her passengers have come ashore in the neighborhood city of Holland, also several trunks and a wooden chest.

The Alpena was built in Marine City in 1866, was 175 feet in length, and 35 feet beam, and measured 654 tons. She was valued at about $75,000 and was insured for $20,000. There are many and various comments regarding her seaworthiness, all of which it may be well to defer until after a thorough investigation, which public opinion and the public good demand.

All who perished have the deep sympathy of this community.

The newspaper reported that bodies were being transported to Zenas G. Winsor's office building, where they were identified, and the remains given to family survivors or friends:

Mrs. S. B. Cole's body, like all others recovered, was only partially dressed. Her body, with that of Montgomery Crossman, was brought into Grand Haven this afternoon, and after it was viewed by the jury in the building in which Mr. Winsor's office is, it was placed in charge of her friends who took it to Muskegon.

Fred Spaeth's body was brought to Grand Haven in a wagon. His body was taken to Grand Rapids by special train on Thursday evening. Edgar T. Locke's body was found washed ashore by Nelson Cooper and Mr. Putnam and brought to the Grand Haven office. It was turned over to Mr. Putnam, who was a friend of the deceased, and he placed the remains in a metallic casket and started for New York, where his parents live in Brooklyn.

The Republican also reported on the steamer Menominee, which weathered the storm and made it safely to the Grand Haven port with all 30 aboard.

The tragedy was about to be depicted in an illustration by Winsor McCay, with the blessing of his teacher, on his classroom blackboard.

Winsor McCay's classroom teacher at Union School at the time was Hattie Capitola Schofield, the 22-year-old daughter of Levin and Mary (Brown) Schofield. Born May 27, 1858 in Farmington, Wisconsin, Schofield lived with her parents in Grand Haven.

Hattie's father, a machinist and inventor, was a creative man possessing drafting and illustration skills. Levin Schofield created many farming implements and devices for the business of corn planting, earning him several patents.

Hattie Schofield became Winsor McCay's teacher in the fall of 1879, replacing teacher Carrie Patchin. Schofield would remain as McCay's instructor until early 1881.

In the 1880 school year, 205 students were enrolled at Union School. Winsor McCay's classroom was in A Room of Union School, a grade range that numbered 61. Two daily sessions that number in half. Besides Miss Schofield, other teachers included Josie Gray in B Room, Jennie Clydesdale in C Room and Hattie Richardson in E Room. D Room was a common area for study and events. The school Principal was Augustus W. Taylor.

While Winsor was clearly the most creative student in his classroom, academic achievement in studies went to fellow "Honor Roll" classmates Albert More, Albert Osterhoff, George Hogkins, Bessie Kay, Jessie Bates, Jennie Steele, Alice Keeler and Minnie Trelor.

While art teachers are not unusual in modern day Ottawa County public schools, they didn't exist in classrooms of young McCay's era. However, in McCay's case, there was an incredible exception.

Prior to accepting a position as a teacher at Union School, Schofield attended Michigan State Normal School in Ypsilanti, Michigan. She graduated in 1879 with a degree in Language, specializing in English and Latin. But language was not her greatest love, it was art.

Schofield was a professional portrait artist. She wasn't a novice who drew and painted for recreational purposes, it was a profession she advertised. Schofield had a solid reputation with many clients throughout Ottawa County, and some in neighboring Kent.

With the permission of his teacher, Hattie C. Schofield, Winsor McCay, at the age of 13 created an illustration of the sinking of the Alpena, using the entire classroom blackboard as a canvas. The drawing showed the steamer battling high winds and waves in Lake Michigan, on October 16.

What is interesting beyond the image's depiction is the fact that McCay was using white chalk on a black surface. Unlike pencil or black ink on white paper, the young artist applied chalk to the bright areas and less, or no chalk, in darker or black areas of the illustration.

Winsor McCay didn't have a photo of the ship at hand when he created the illustration, he employed a technique he had developed in youth called "memory drawing." Later in life, McCay stated that close observation, and a cognitive process, gave him the ability to achieve remarkable accuracy in a drawing when the subject was not present.

In 1880, photography was still rare and was an expensive technique at the time. Few photos of the Alpena were ever taken. In fact, McCay's drawing is one of only two known surviving illustrations depicting the Alpena disaster.

All of Union School's students and teachers, as well as many citizens of Spring Lake, visited A Room to see McCay's dramatic illustration.

It was so impressive that an area photographer was summoned and took a photograph of the masterpiece. This photographic image of the McCay illustration was offered for sale as prints as a keepsake observing the tragedy.

Winsor McCay earned a percentage from the photographic prints of his work, thus making *The Sinking of The Alpena* his first commercial artwork.

In John Canemaker's book about Winsor McCay, a man named H. A. Woods recalled Winsor McCay's classroom illustration of The Alpena. He described it in Canemaker's book:

"Winsor here drew a picture of the wreck as he imagined it on the blackboard in our school. A photographer heard about it, and came over to the

school, took a picture of it, then sold the pictures."

The man, Harry A. Wood, the only son of Alexander and Ella Wood, was age six at the time.

Young McCay's first published work wasn't anything to celebrate due to its tragic subject matter, but it undoubtedly resonated with Winsor McCay at the time that art could become a profession.

One can just imagine the McCay, who once said he didn't care if folks liked his work or not, now entertaining the thought, "Do you mean I can make money doing this?"

McCay's drawing of the Alpena shows the steamer on a tilt, revealing the fittings and mechanics atop the ship. These match actual photographs showing the top level of the vessel. Thus, there is little doubt as to whether Winsor McCay was ever onboard the Alpena, at port, under the escort of Zenas G. Winsor.

When existing photographs of the Alpena are compared to McCay's illustration it reveals details atop the steamer that are visible only if one were standing on the top deck of the ship. This would not have been visible from the dock while the ship was moored at port.

The drama concerning the tragedy of the Alpena would continue on for a year, as the Goodrich Transportation Company was sued by many families who lost loved ones.

During an inquiry into the tragedy, it was discovered that even though the Goodrich line renovated the ship five years earlier, it was known to be in disrepair and unsafe in high seas.

In January 1881, newspapers across the country reported the result of an inquest into the sinking of the Alpena, which was conducted in Grand Haven. In conclusion, it was designated that the Goodrich Transportation Company was liable for the loss of nearly 80 lives. One such report explains this:

The result of the inquest held in Grand Haven, Michigan, over the victims of the wreck of the steamer Alpena is a verdict censuring the Goodrich Transportation Company. They found that The Alpena was unseaworthy, her life preservers unfit for use, her lifeboats rotten, and her crew inexperienced sailors.

How much of this Zenas G. Winsor was aware of regarding the inexperience of her crew, vessel condition and the state of life-saving accessories is unknown. But others interviewed who worked at the Grand Haven port, and who knew of the Alpena, agreed that she "wasn't safe" to put out into storm.

Zenas G. Winsor was subpoenaed during the inquest. He was questioned and testified in court, in regards to civil suits filed by the families of deceased parties.

The Goodrich Transportation Company was actively engaged in the ongoing legal process, not only to recover financial losses regarding the ship and its cargo, but they also hired a Chicago attorney to limit the benefits, or punitive damages, for claimants who had lost someone in the disaster.

Debris and artifacts of the vessel would continue to wash ashore at Ottawa and Allegan County for the next three decades.

In the end, Zenas G. Winsor was not held responsible for any loss of life, nor was he charged with any safety violation. But it was a nightmare he would never forget. And it goes without saying that the entire experience made a lasting impression on Winsor McCay, that influenced his 1917 animated cartoon later in life, *The Sinking of the Lusitania*.

In the book *The History of Ottawa County*, published two years later, Zenas G. Winsor was mentioned in regards to The Alpena tragedy. It stated that "Z. G. Winsor was an agent for the Goodrich boats, unfortunately for the Alpena."

Winsor McCay created illustrations of many ships and boats while hanging out at the Grand Haven port. He also drew boats loading lumber and goods at sawmills near his Spring Lake home.

Currently, a search in Spring Lake and Grand Haven for other Winsor McCay illustrations is ongoing, but nothing new has been uncovered. The search includes illustrations of Spring Lake landmarks and everyday life that would have been created by young McCay.

An effort to locate textbooks that would have been used at Union School during that period has also been engaged, to see if any contain Winsor McCay sketches in the margins.

Imagine finding an original, signed childhood "Winsor Z. McKay" illustration today. It would be the holy grail of comics history.

Two first generation prints struck from the negative of *The Sinking of The Alpena* illustration by Winsor McCay are stored away in the collection of the Tri-Cities Historical Museum of Grand Haven.

What follows is McCay's drawing, taken from 800 .dpi scans of the 1880 prints, available for the first time to the general public since the young artist created it at the age of 13.

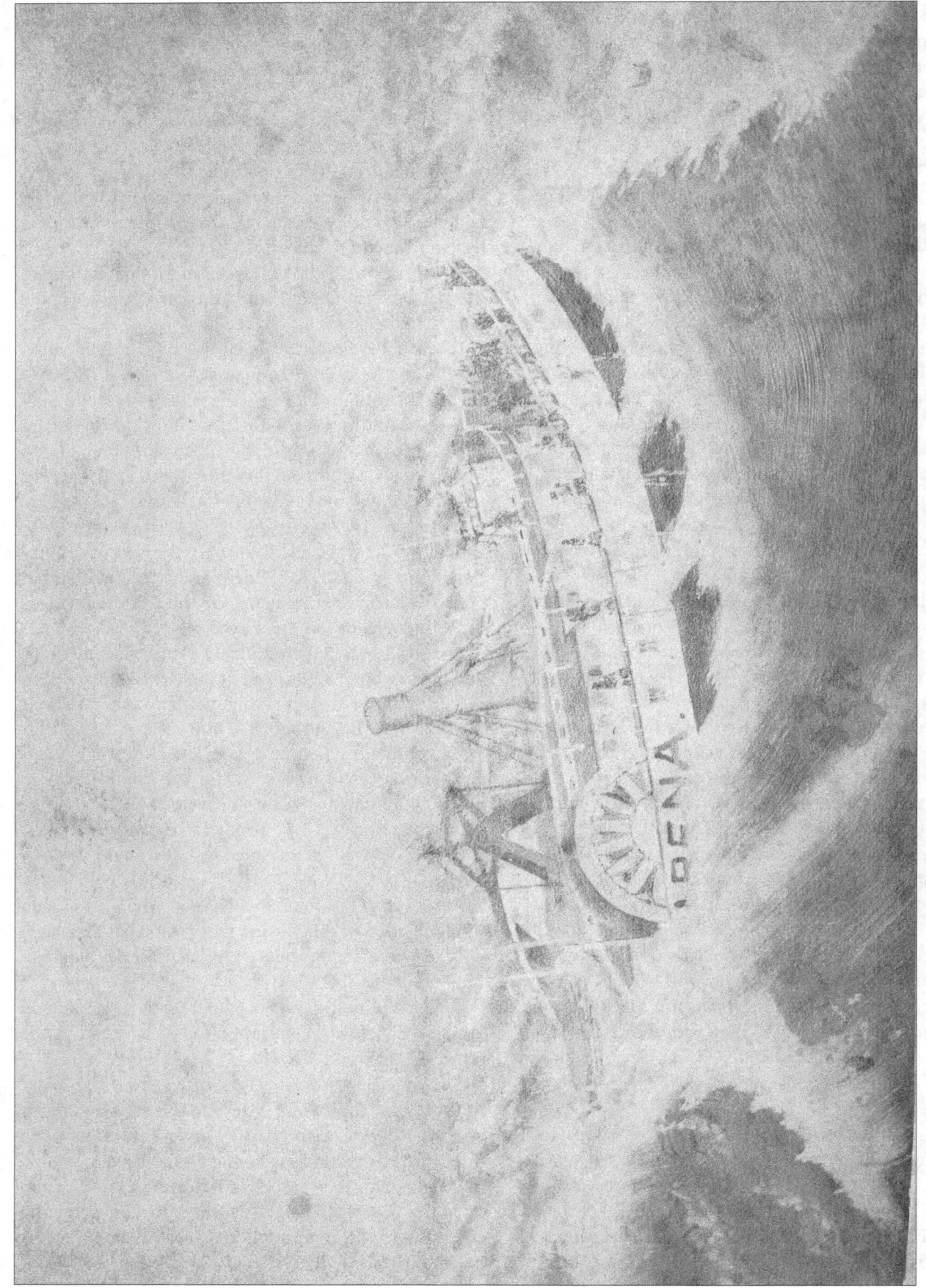

THE SINKING OF THE ALPENA PHOTO "PRINT A"

The Tri-Cities Museum of Ottawa County, Michigan, has two different prints of Winsor McCay's chalkboard illustration of *The Sinking of The Alpena*. While struck from the same negative, Print A shows more detail, but is spotted with dozens of age marks. Museum Collection Manager Meredith Slover explained each print "aged a little differently." The above image is cropped.

THE SINKING OF THE ALPENA PHOTO "PRINT B"

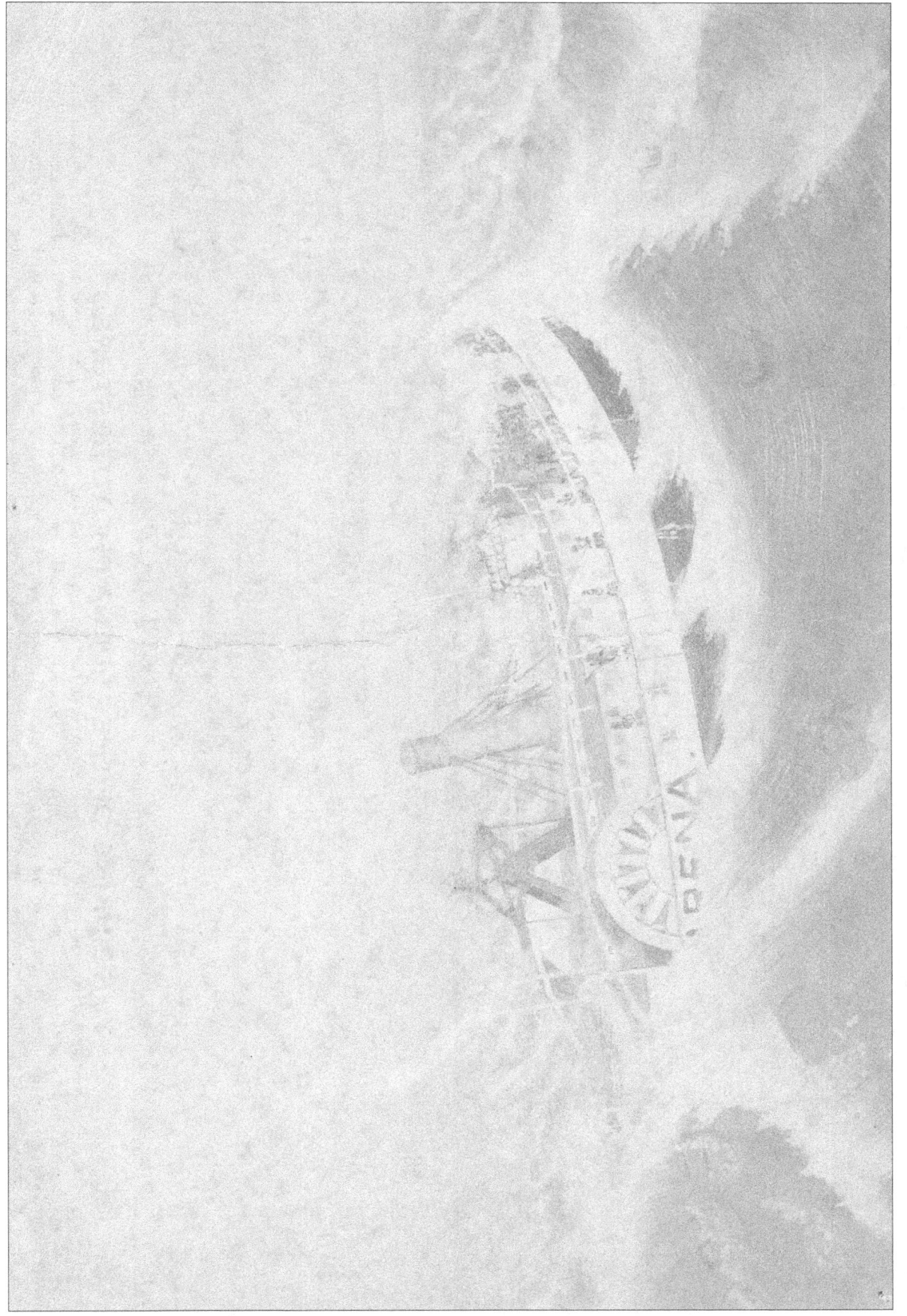

The second photo, Print B, of Winsor McCay's chalkboard illustration *The Sinking of The Alpena*, on file at the Tri-Cities Museum, in Ottawa County, Michigan. While struck from the same negative, Image B (above) is a bit lighter, shows less detail, but is clear of age spots. This print, unlike the previous one, is uncropped, showing more of McCay's actual drawing. Since the photographer made prints of McCay's illustration by order, it is not unusual for different photos to show more or less of the drawing, depending on how the negative was enlarged when the print was made. This print was used as the version that is the third image presented in this book, the restored photograph on page 22.

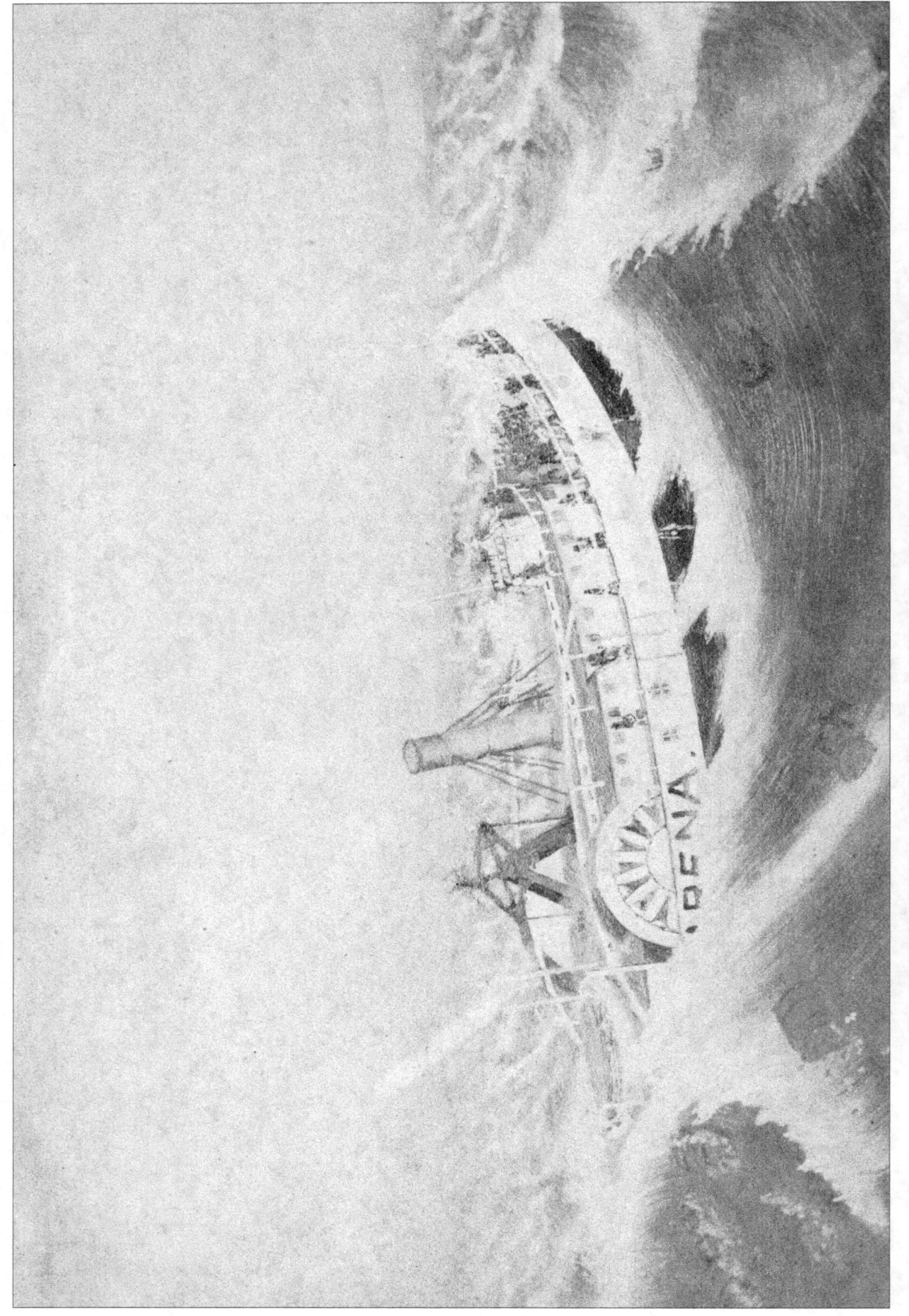

THE SINKING OF THE ALPENA PHOTO RESTORED

Using the original 800 dpi scan of Print B, this digitally restored version of Winsor McCay's chalkboard illustration of *The Sinking of The Alpena* repairs damage, adjusts dark, light and mid-tones, and also sharpens the image to present the best possible reproduction. Several names associated with photography during the period have been researched, yet it is uncertain as to which individual took the picture. The negative of the photo does not exist. It is possible other copies of the McCay illustration are in an attic or buried folder in a private residence, but only two are known to exist, both of which are at the museum. The clarity of the original, upon high magnification, reveals the surface texture of the classroom blackboard.

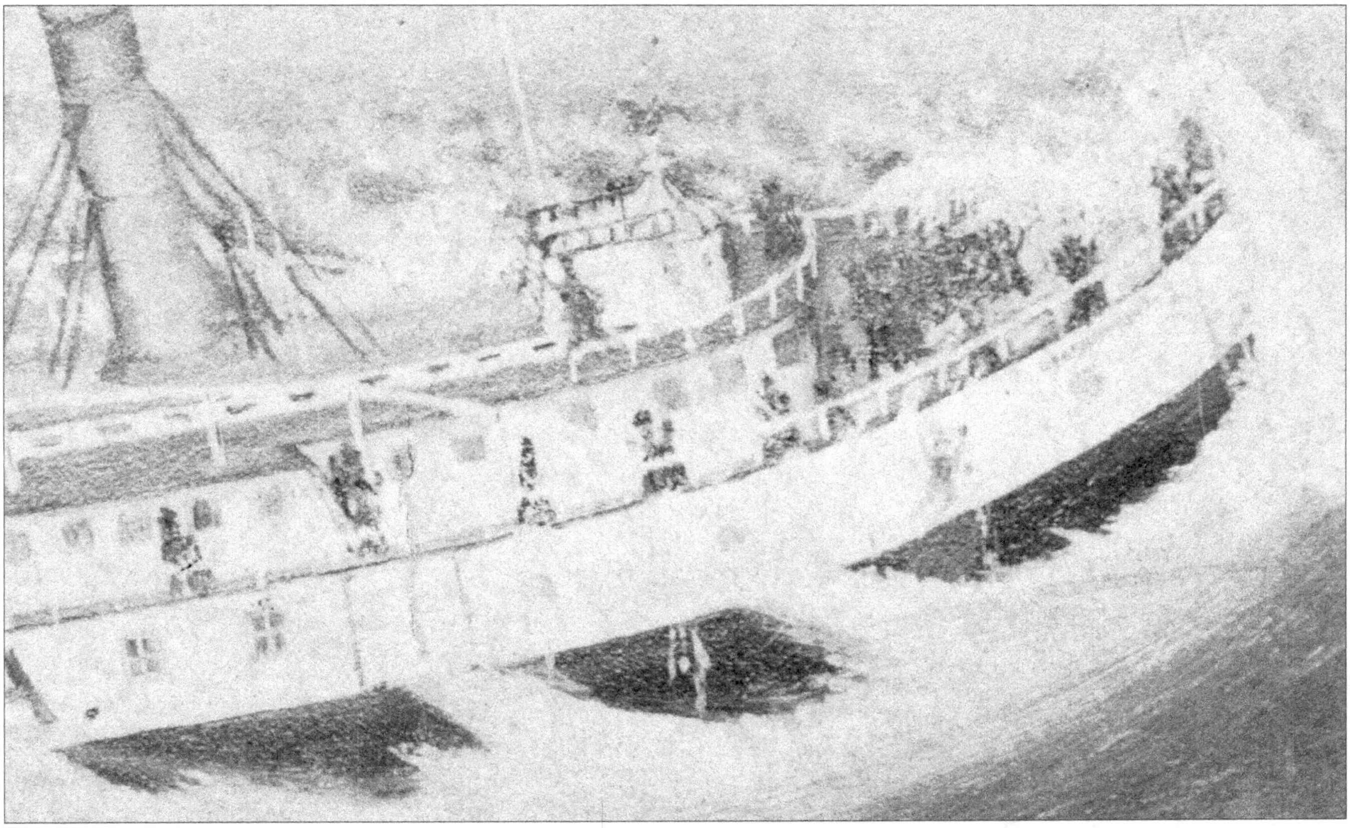

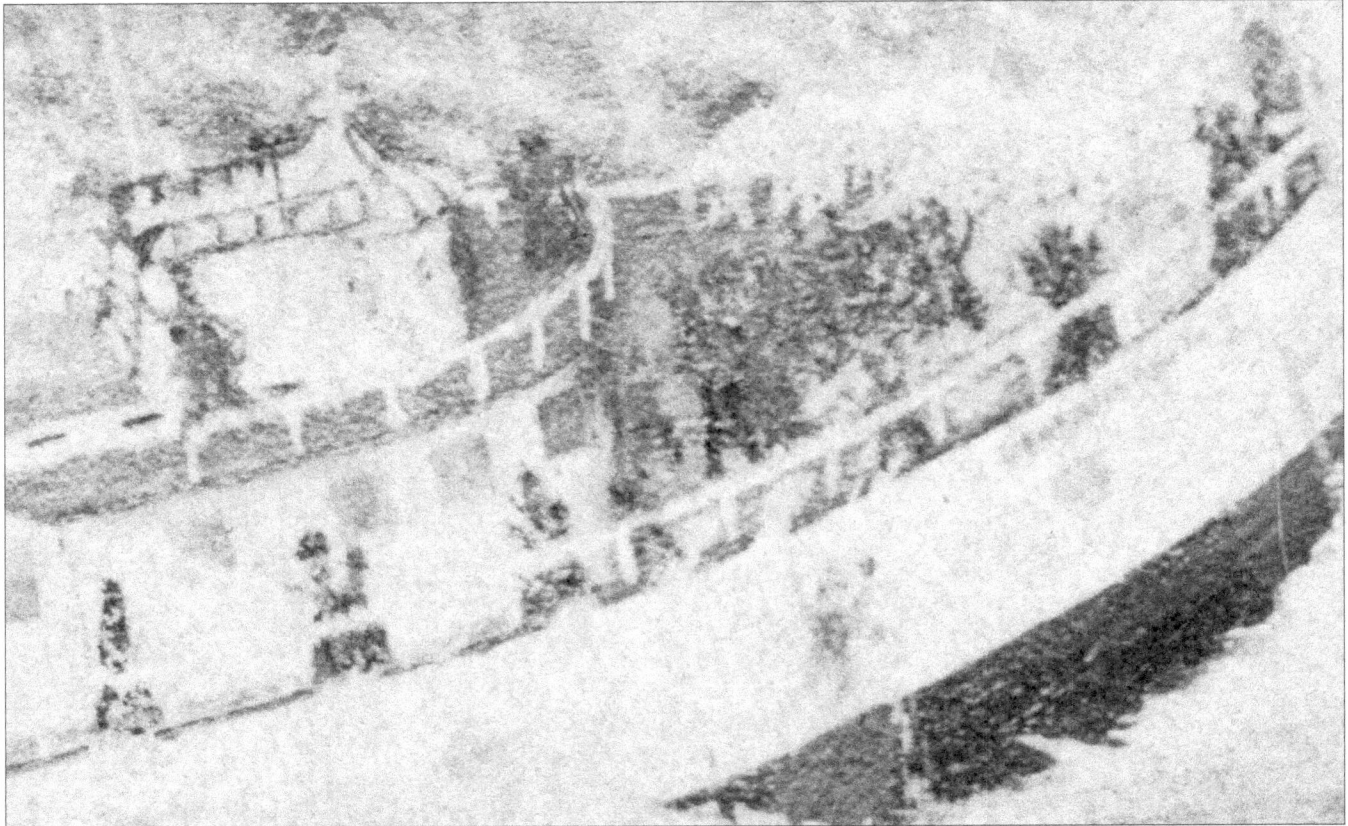

The above cutaway enlargements of the restored version of *The Sinking of The Alpena* illustration reveals details of the crew (upper deck) and passenger's plight, as people scramble for the bow of the sinking ship. The ship's captain, Nelson W. Napier, is depicted in front of the wheelhouse.

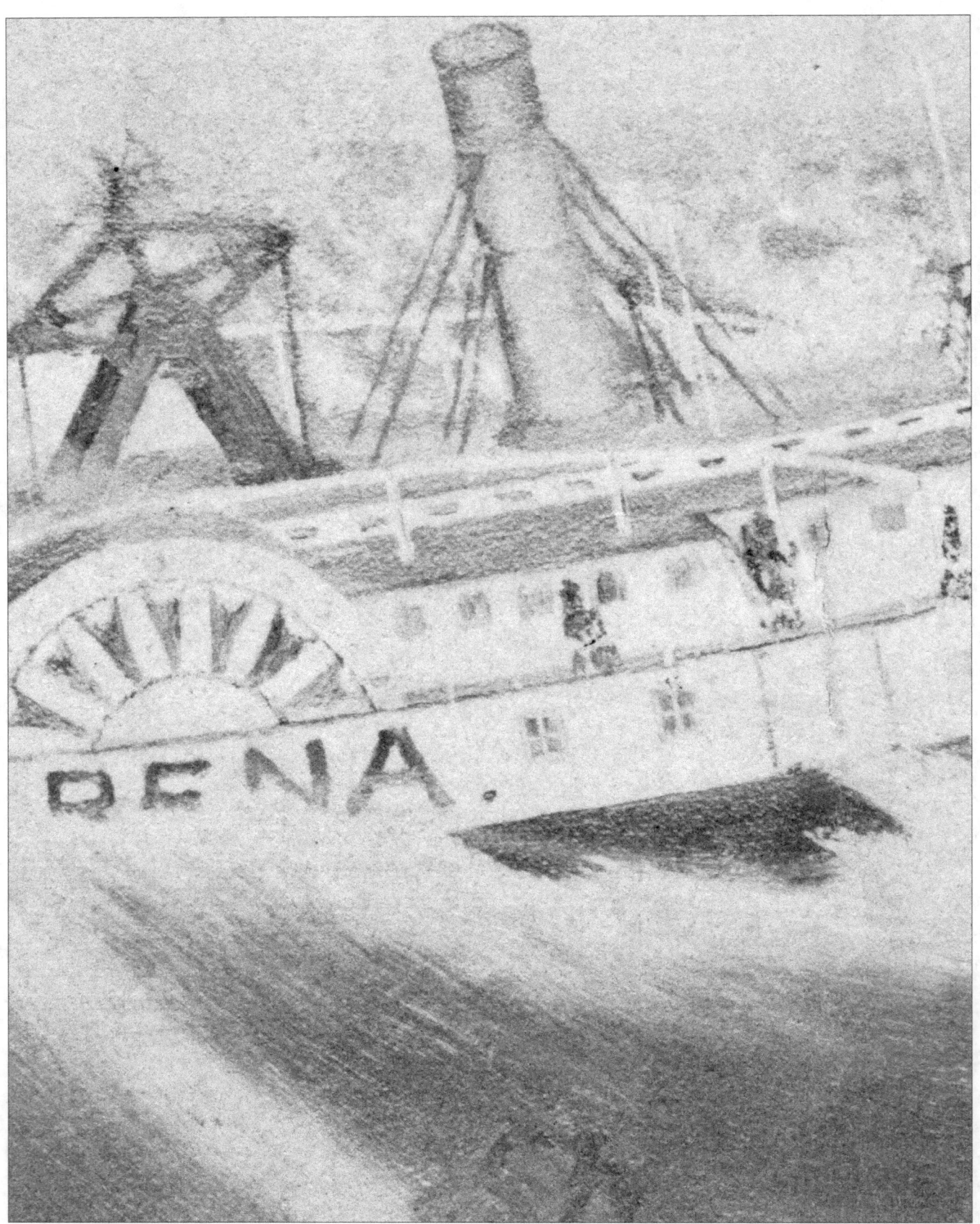

The above cutaway enlargement of the restored version of *The Sinking of The Alpena* illustration reveals details of Winsor McCay's white chalk strokes, and shading, to create the work. Areas such as the smokestack, lines attached, rigging, around the paddle-wheel and windows show McCay's use of charcoal to create crisp, black outlines.

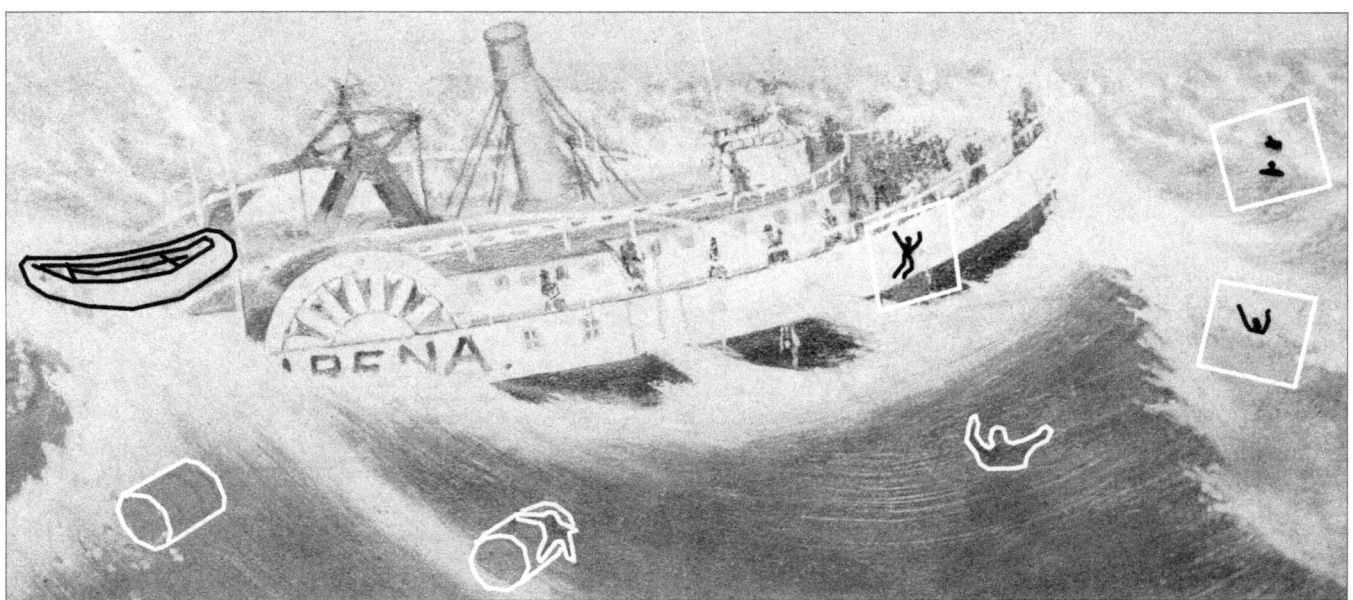

Restored version of *The Sinking of The Alpena* illustration reveals astounding detail. From upper left to right: A lifeboat is washed off the stern of the ship, among the debris is a barrel, then another barrel with a person clinging to it, a passenger jumps from the railing off the ship, and two passengers are depicted with their arms upward in the raging water. At top, the ship passengers scramble toward the bow. Below, some of those images without highlight outlines.

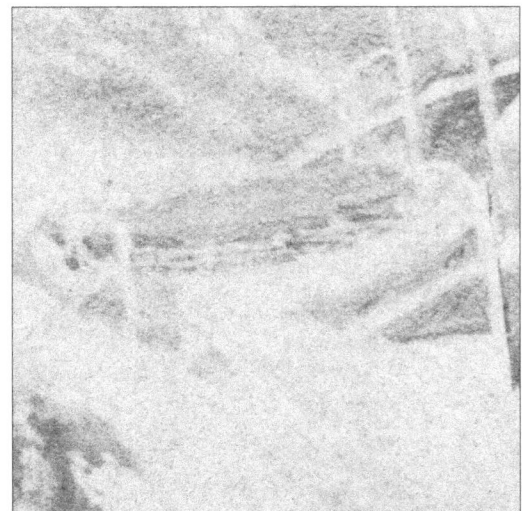 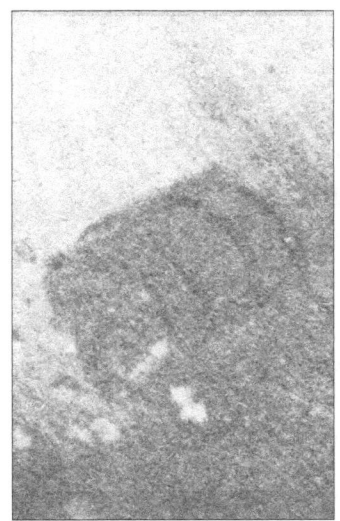 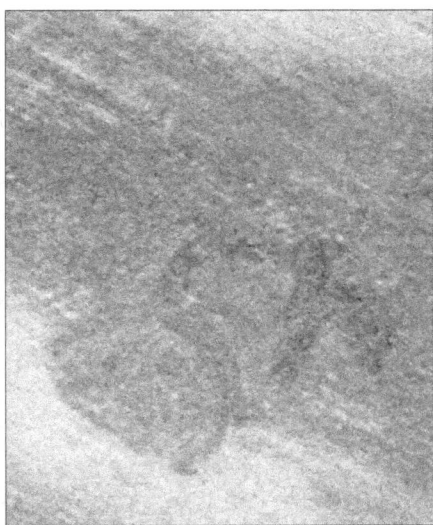

Left to right: Lifeboat washed off the stern, barrel floating in the water, man clinging to barrel in the water.

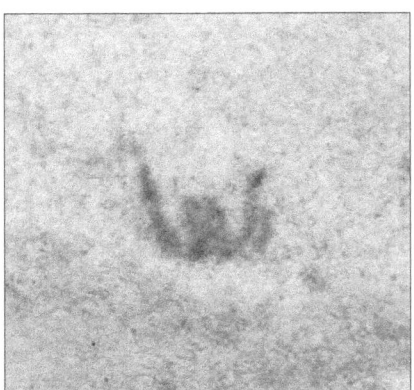 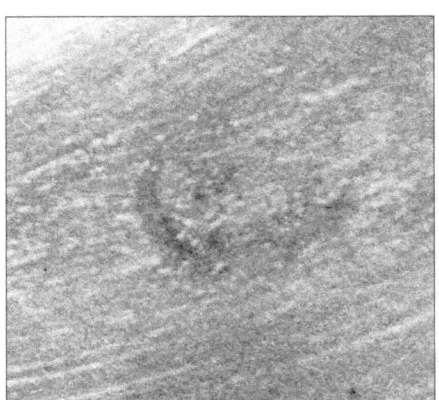 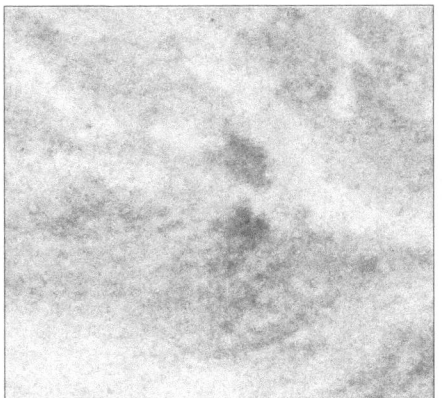

Left to right: Passenger overboard, passenger overboard, two passengers beside each other in the water.

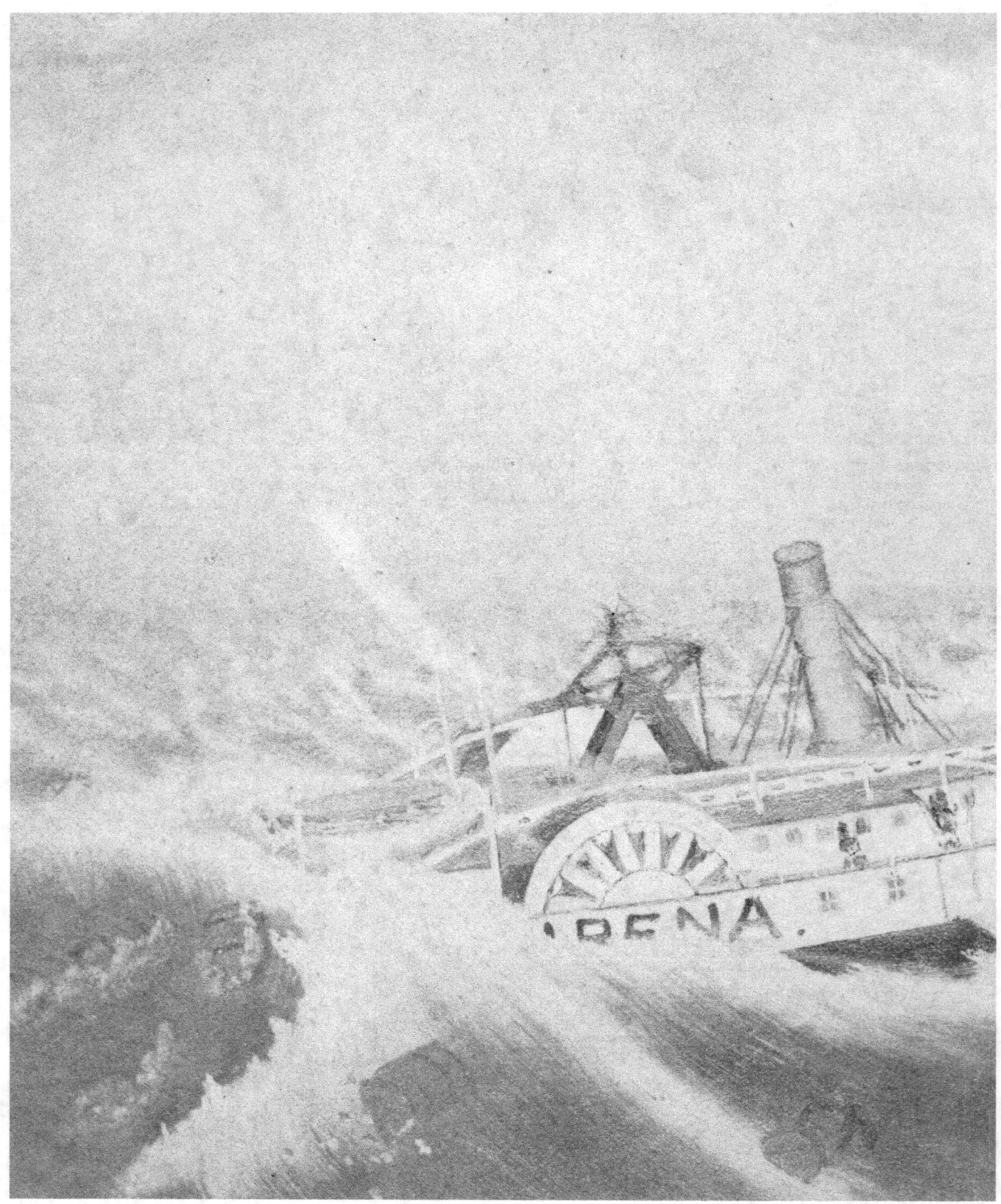

THE SINKING OF THE ALPENA LEFT SIDE
There is no measurements as to how large the blackboard was in Winsor McCay's classroom when he created *The Sinking of The Alpena*. Some standards in place, circa 1880, set the width of a board between 28-36 inches, according to age of students in the room. There was also a standard of chalk rails being 24-28 inches off the classroom floor.

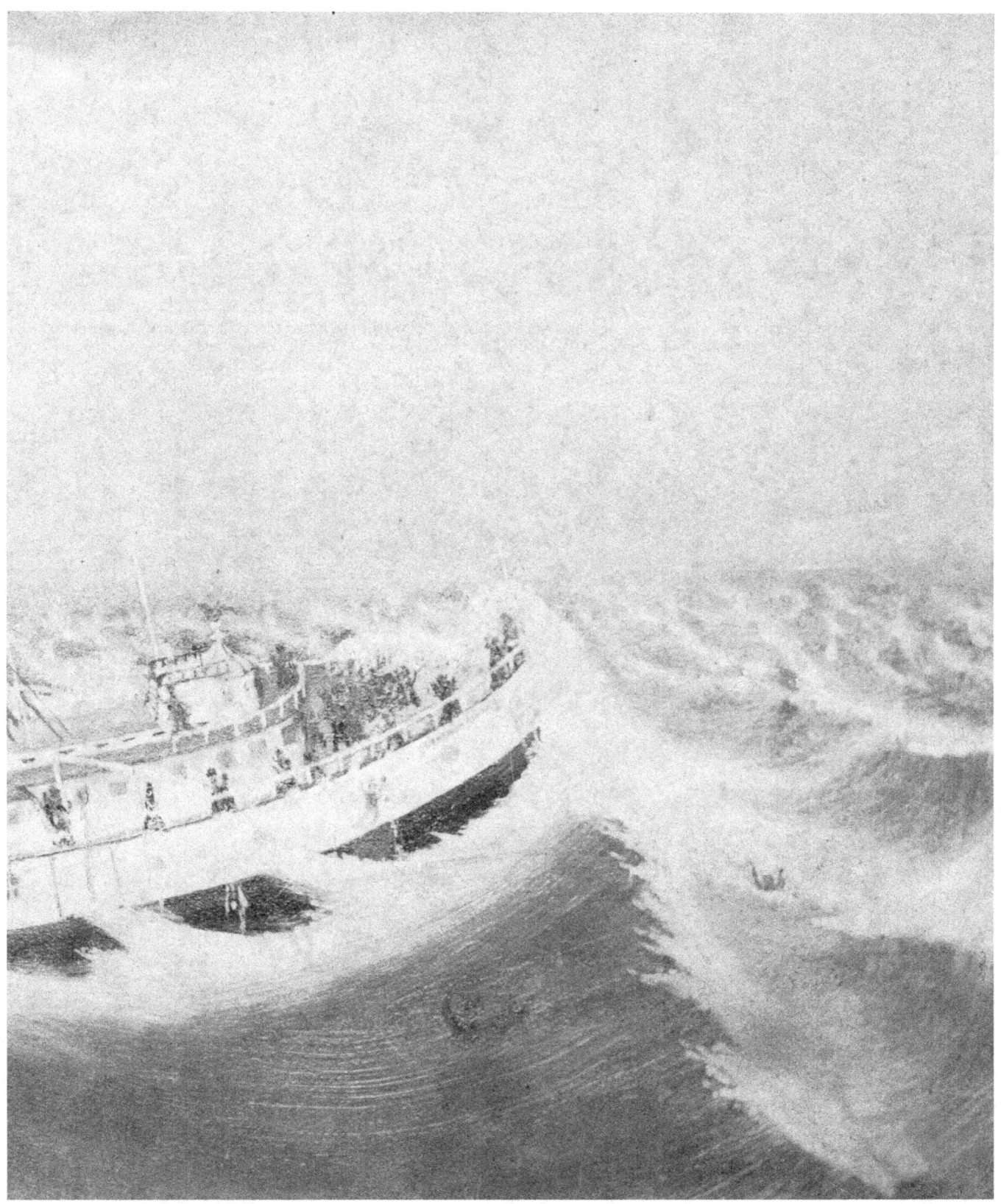

THE SINKING OF THE ALPENA RIGHT SIDE
Recognizing the widths and height on the previous page, it is likely McCay's classroom had a chalkboard 36 inches in width. The chalk rail likely began 26 inches off the floor. The horizon and ship appear halfway down the board because anything higher was out of the boy's reach. He likely stood on a stool or chair to complete the upper ship and sky. As an adult, Winsor McCay barely stood 5 feet tall.

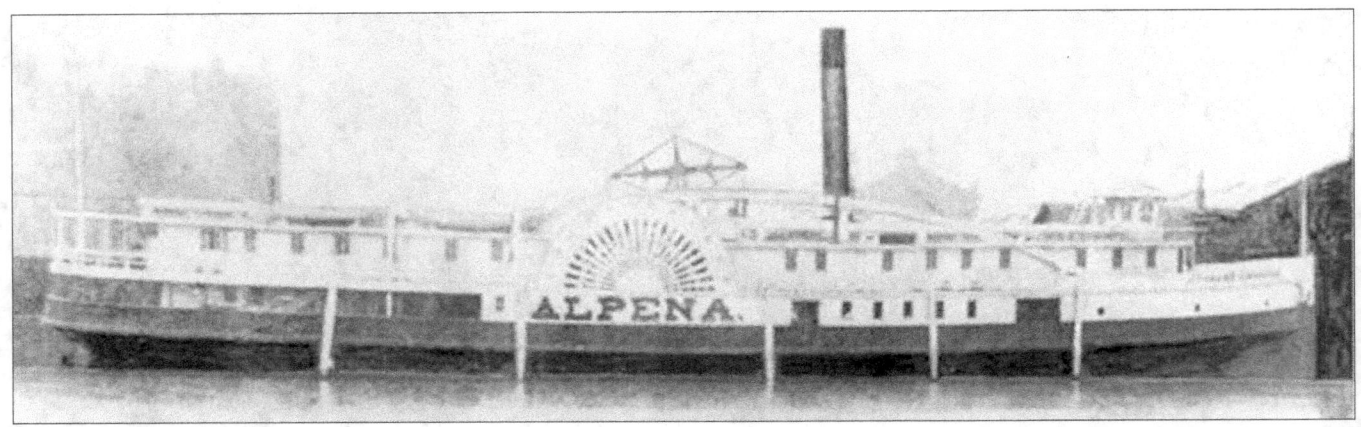

Few photos exist of the actual vessel Alpena, one of which appears above. Below is the Winsor McCay illustration. Underneath is the above photo of the Alpena, altered to a similar perspective and angle, and placed within McCay's curling waves artwork. When comparing the below illustration with the bottom picture, and adding an actual photographic image of the ship, one can see young Winsor McCay not only possessed an amazing memory of the steamship, but was able to essentially replicate it.

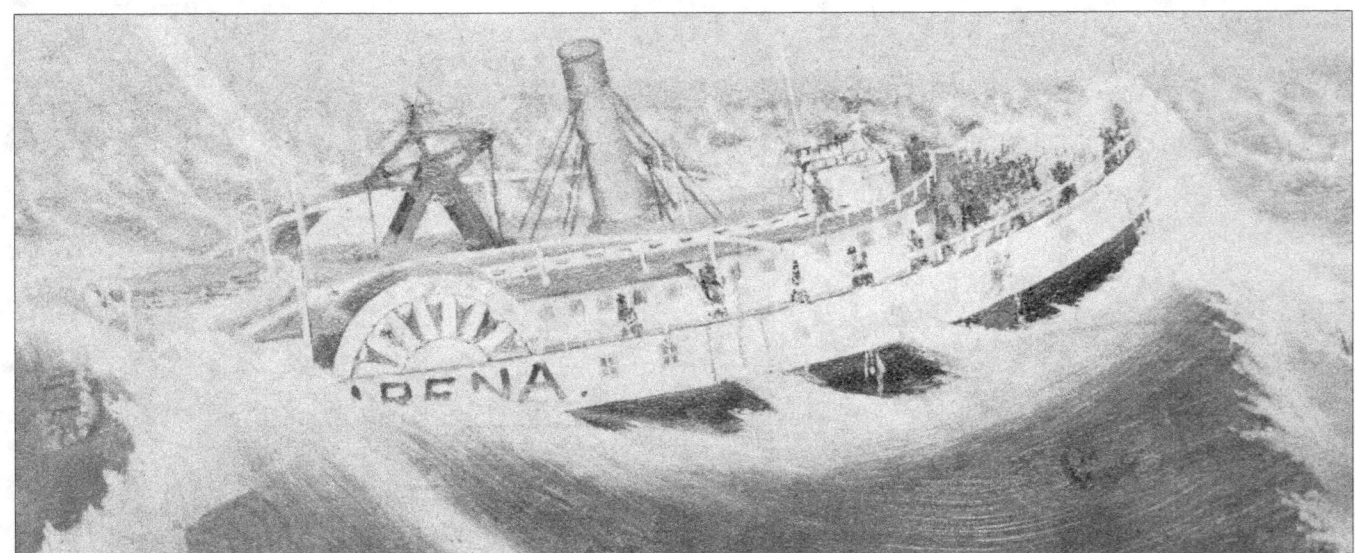

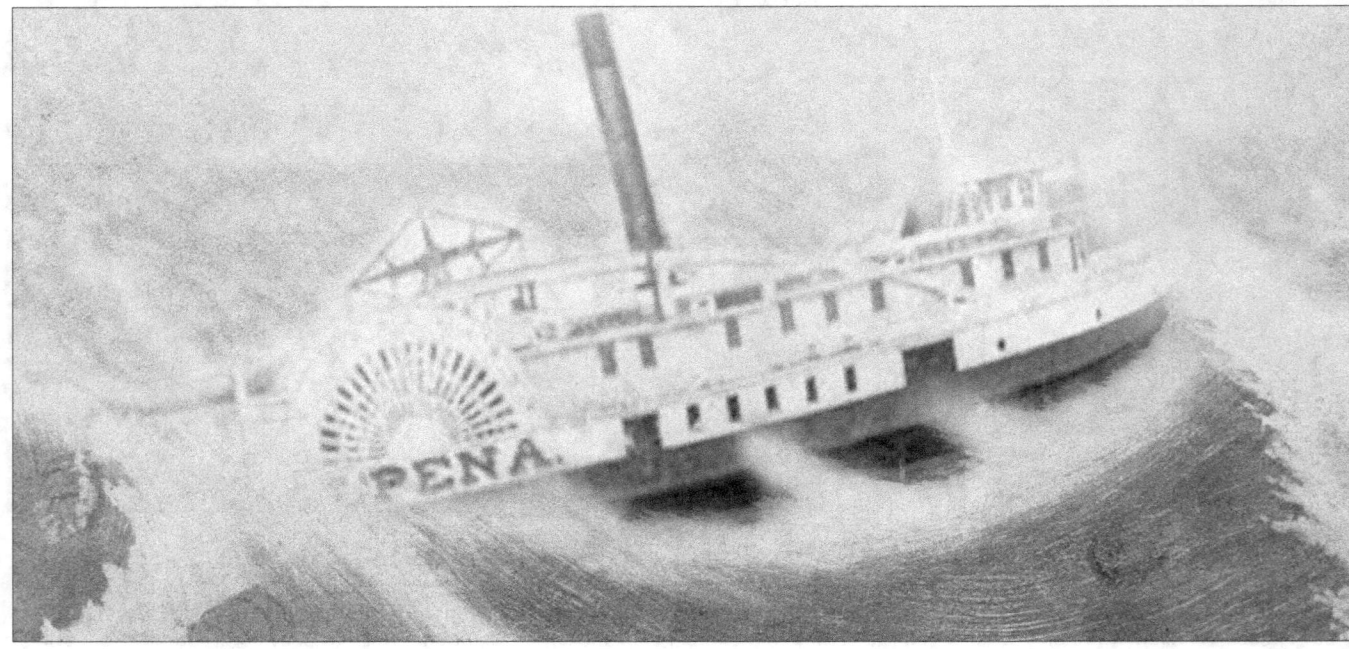

WINSOR McCAY MOVES ON
Departs Spring Lake At The Age Of 18

After gaining recognition as an artist with the circulation of *The Sinking of The Alpena* illustration, McCay continued to draw the sights of his hometown, Spring Lake. Vessels, wagons and sleds in winter loading up lumber from area sawmills became subjects of his art, as well as the machinery that cut the logs.

As a teen, Winsor McCay would take a job at an area sawmill for a period, but was more interested in boats. This drew the attention of William M. Barrett, who was jumpstarting a small business constructing clinker boats.

Winsor assumed a job with Barrett, and was now putting together boats – even though they were rowboats – to earn money.

Clinker boats was a practice of building boats where the edges of planks overlapped, much like clapboard on a home. The planks were also joined end to end to a stake. The boats routinely had round bottoms and copper, or iron, rivets were used as fasteners. Adhesives and nails were used, as well, and completed boats were varnished and sometimes painted.

The appealing aspect of the job was that a clinker boat design employed the same method used by Norsemen, which likely fascinated the teenage McCay. The craftsmanship alone was that of a work of art. Winsor likely got to do some custom paint jobs, too.

The fledgling effort by Barrett was located just a few convenient blocks west of the McCay home. Cutler and Savidge sawmill supplied the cut the planks used to construct the boats. William Barrett had worked for that sawmill before developing an interest in boat building.

Barrett was a friend of Robert McCay, as well, as both were Masons and members of the Spring Lake Masonic Lodge.

Barrett, who was just shy of age 30 at the time, became Vice President of the Clinker Boat Company, officially established in 1887, two years after the McCays departed Spring Lake.

Robert McCay, with the help of Aloys Bilz, had been dabbling in the field of real estate. Evidence exists that he likely was an agent for Bilz, or a realtor, at the time he packed up his family and moved in 1885.

That year the McCay family moved from Spring Lake to the town of Stanton, Michigan, about 40 miles northwest of Spring Lake. And, the rest is history.

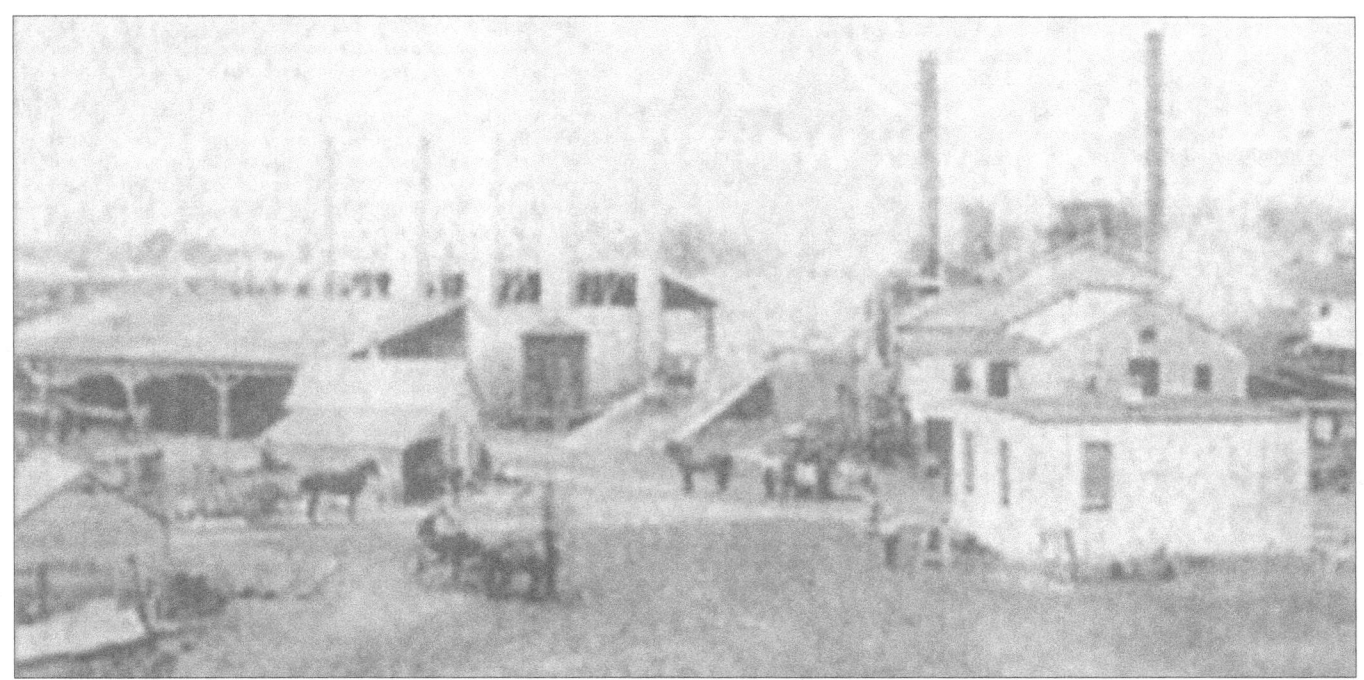

Winsor McCay as a teen worked at a sawmill, and for William M. Barrett during the establishment of what became The Spring Lake Clinker Boat Manufacturing Company. McCay assembled the rowboats for the company. The photograph shows the business as it grew, eventually becoming the Barrett Boat Works, still in business today.

WINSOR McCAY TIMELINE
Found On The Spring Lake District Library Website

1867-1903: Michigan, Chicago, Cincinnati and Developing His Skills

Jan. 8, 1866 Marriage of Robert and Janet (Murray) McKay (Winsor McKay's parents) in West Zorra, Ontario

1866 Robert and Janet move to Spring Lake, MI.

September 26, 1867 Birth of Zenas Winsor McKay (later known as Winsor Z. McCay). The exact date and place of birth are unknown. McCay's tombstone in Brooklyn and the 1910 Census say 1869. McCay himself claimed he was born in 1871, but it's probable he was actually born in 1867 on a visit back to West Zorra.

1880 13 year old McCay draws the sinking of the Goodrich Steamship *Alpena* on the blackboard of the Spring Lake Union School. A picture was taken of the drawing by a professional photographer, and the image was sold on postcards.

1886 At his father's insistence, McCay enrolls in Cleary's Business College in Ypsilanti but spends his time in Detroit at vaudeville shows honing his drawing skills.

1888 McCay is taken on as a student by Michigan State Normal School (Eastern Michigan University) Prof. John Goodison, even though he is not enrolled in the school. This is the only formal art instruction McCay ever received.

1889 McCay and a friend move to Chicago, where he plans to study at the Art Institute. He does not enroll, but finds employment as an apprentice at the National Printing and Engraving Company. Much of his work is designing and drawing fanciful posters for traveling circuses.

1891 McCay moves to Cincinnati and works for the Vine Street Dime Museum, a "freak show," where he drew the dog-faced boy, the bearded lady and other attractions.

1891 Maude Leonore Dufour, age 14, visits the Dime Museum and McCay is captivated by her. After a whirlwind courtship, the two elope to Covington, KY and are married by a Justice of the Peace.

Mac, as he was then known, begins drawing advertisements for the *Cincinnati Commercial Tribune* while working for the Dime Museum.

1900 McCay moves to the *Cincinnati Enquirer*, where he produces his first comic strip, *The Tales of the Jungle Imps* by Felix Fiddle. The strip ran from January 11-November 9, 1903.

1903-1911: New York, Comic Strips, Vaudeville and Broadway

1903 McCay moves to New York to take a position at the *New York Herald* (and also draws for its sister paper, the *New York Evening Telegram*)

1904 A run of short comic strips in the *Herald* and *Telegram*: *Mr. Goodenough*, *Little Sister's Beau* and *The Phurious Phinish of Phoolish Philipe's Phunny Phrolics* allow McCay to further explore this new art form.

Little Sammy Sneeze, McCay's new serial strip with a child protagonist, debuts in the *Herald* and runs from July 24, 1904-December 9, 1906.

September 10, 1904 marks the first appearance the comic strip that would establish McCay as the premiere comic illustrator of his time, *Dream of the Rarebit Fiend*. He publishes it under the pseudonym, "Silas." With an interruption during 1911-1913, this strip runs until August 3, 1913, first in the *Telegram* and then the *Herald*.

1905 The short run comic, *The Story of Hungry Henrietta*, debuts in the *Herald* on January 8, 1905 and runs through July 16 of that year.

In the same year, McCay introduces a unique strip, *A Pilgrim's Progress* by Mister Bunion, in the *Telegram*. It is based on the 17th century Christian classic, *The Pilgrim's Progress*, by John Bunyan. It will run through December 18, 1910.

McCay's best known and most beloved comic strip, *Little Nemo in Slumberland*, first appears in the *Herald* on October 15, 1905 and runs through April 23, 1911. McCay will take Nemo with him when he leaves the *Herald*, and in all, the young dreamer will continue to have adventures in various papers through December 16, 1926. *Little Nemo's* lovable characters also inspire McCay's first attempts at moving animation.

1906 McCay begins doing chalk lightning sketches – a popular attraction performed by artists – on the Vaudeville circuit. A natural performer, McCay's act is wildly successful. His fame increases as he travels the circuit east of the Mississippi through 1917.

1908 After a one-week preview run in Philadelphia, the lavish musical, *Little Nemo,* opens October 20 on Broadway. It runs there and in other eastern cities through the winter of 1910.

1911-1924 : Animated Films and the Hearst Papers

1911 McCay's first attempt at animation, *Little Nemo*, astonishes his Vaudeville audiences, who see beloved characters from the comic strip jump, flip, expand, contract, smoke cigars, roll their eyes and otherwise come to life.

With his contract expiring at the *Herald*, McCay makes the move to William Randolph Hearst's newspaper empire.

1912 McCay's second animated film, *How a Mosquito Operates*, and its slightly anthropomorphic mosquito protagonist charms enthusiastic audiences.

1914 After a two-year wait, audiences are rewarded with the endearing *Gertie the Dinosaur*. Invested with human characteristics like shyness, a temper and the ability to cry when her feelings were hurt, Gertie becomes an immediate audience favorite.

This time period was the heyday of Yellow Journalism, and Hearst's papers were in a war of ideas, words and images with those of Joseph Pulitzer. The spoils of that war were dollars – millions upon millions of them. During the first three months of the year, McCay entirely ceased drawing comics to concentrate solely on editorial cartoons to accompany the papers' often inflammatory op-ed pieces.

1918 McCay makes the very first foray into serious subject matter in animation, *The Sinking of the Lusitania*. The film brings viewers to the site of the tragedy off the West coast of Ireland on May 17, 1915, when the ship, in route from Liverpool to New York, was torpedoed by a German submarine. The somber, serious material and respectful way McCay treats the subject opens up vast horizons of possibility for new directions in animated film.

1918-21 *The Centaurs, Flip's Circus,* and *Gertie on Tour* were short films that were never commercially distributed, but were featured in McCay's vaudeville act. By this time, his audiences had come to expect that a film short would be part of a McCay performance.

1921 McCay's final three films, *Bug Vaudeville, The Pet* and *The Flying House*, were based on his successful comic strip, *Dreams of the Rarebit Fiend*. In the films, McCay provides innovative subject matter, characters and techniques that would inspire animators for decades.

1922 McCay makes an arrangement with the B.F. Keith Vaudeville circuit to continue booking performances for him, in New York and other cities east of the Mississippi. His act had sometimes been a source of conflict with William Randolph Hearst in the past, but the two must have come to an agreement when McCay took a forced vacation at Hearst's ranch in San Simeon, CA in 1920. These performances were a welcome escape from the steady and intense pressure Hearst put on McCay.

1924-1934: The Final Decade

1924 McCay leaves the Hearst papers when his contract expires and returns to his former employer, now the *New York Herald Tribune*. That year, he is invited to revive the *Little Nemo in Slumberland* comic strip after thirteen years away from drawing strips. Having escaped the demands of Hearst and his editor, McCay's imagination and creativity were revitalized with this last run of *Nemo,* which ended December 26, 1926.

1927 After a few years of wooing by Hearst, McCay returns to draw for him again. McCay claims the move was because of personal admiration for Hearst, but the *Herald Tribune's* decision to drop Nemo undoubtedly influenced his decision. McCay returns to drawing editorial cartoons, and the pressure on him from Hearst's editor is more intense than ever.

1921-34 Though McCay had plans to work on further films, including projects with his son, Robert, William Randolph Hearst refused to allow McCay the time off he requested to focus on animation. Hearst had relied heavily on McCay to produce biting and pointed editorial and political cartoons for his papers since McCay started working for him. As the years went by, Hearst saw McCay's work as deteriorating in both artistic acumen and wit, and he often focused his mercurial temper on the artist. McCay continued to draw for Hearst until his death on July 26, 1934, with his last editorial cartoon being published four days before he passed.

www.ingramcontent.com/pod-product-compliance
Lightning Source LLC
Chambersburg PA
CBHW082224220526
45470CB00010B/3305